MOUNTAIN COOKIN
BUTTER
BUTTER

Puddin' & Pie

A Reborn Studios Publication

ART DESIGN
Saba Shafiq
BookCoversPro.com

EDITOR
Missy Jones

ASSISTANT EDITORS
Roger Jones
McKenzie Jones
James Berger
Debbie Berger

PRODUCTION MANAGER
Brian Berger

Published in the United States by Reborn Studios
1664 Frogtown Rd, #1174, Union, Kentucky 41091

ISBN 978-1-965277-04-1

Printed in China.

Puddin' & Pie

A Mother-Daughter Collection of Favorite and New Baking Recipes

By Missy & Kenzie Jones

TABLE OF CONTENTS

COOKIES/BARS/BROWNIES

BREADS

LOW CARB/LOW SUGAR SWEETS

CAKES/PIES/FROSTINGS

DESSERTS

CANDIES/FUDGE

Forward

Some of my sweetest memories from growing up in the Appalachian Mountains were made right in the kitchen, baking alongside my mommy. She taught me so much — how to roll out biscuits just right by hand, how to tell they were done by their smell, and most importantly, that baking is a way to show love. It was her love language, and she passed it down to me.

When I became a mother myself, I knew I wanted to share those same moments with Kenzie — the joy of baking from scratch, the laughter through flour-covered messes, and the tradition of using food to bring family together and create lasting memories.

That's why this little book means so much to me. It's called Puddin' and Pie — not only for all the sweet treats inside, but because "Puddin'" has always been my nickname for Kenzie. Every recipe holds a memory, and every page is filled with love from both of us.

Our hope is that this cookbook brings a little sweetness into your home — and helps you make some special memories of your own.

Missy

Forward

My earliest memories in the kitchen go back to when I was about six or seven years old. My mom would sit me on the counter beside her mixer, and I'd help her make her classic buttercream frosting. I might have only measured out the powdered sugar or poured in the vanilla, but those moments in the kitchen with my momma sparked a lifelong love of baking and created memories I'll always cherish.

My mom is my best friend, and baking has always been one of our favorite things to do together. In Appalachia, food has a way of bringing people together. Every funeral, church service, birthday party, and family gathering is followed by a meal fit for a king. I'm so grateful for the chance to share a little piece of that tradition — and our culture — with you and your family through this baking book.

As you make the recipes inside, I hope your kitchen fills with love, sweet aromas, delicious treats, and memories to last a lifetime. lifetime.

McKenzie

Cookies/Bars/ Brownies

Brown Butter Chocolate Chip Cookies

Ingredients

- 2¼ c all purpose-flour
- 1 tsp baking soda
- 16 Tbsp *(2 sticks)* unsalted butter
- 1½ c dark brown sugar
- ¼ c granulated sugar
- 1 large egg + 1 additional yolk, all at room temperature
- 1 Tbsp vanilla extract
- 1 Tbsp sour cream
- 1 c semi-sweet chocolate chips
- 1 c milk chocolate chips
- ½ c toasted pecans or walnuts *(optional)*

Directions

1. First, brown the butter by adding butter to a large saucepan and place over medium heat. (16 tbsp unsalted butter)
2. The butter will begin to sizzle and then eventually foam. Make sure you whisk constantly during this process.
3. After a couple minutes, the butter will begin to brown and turn a golden amber color on the bottom of the saucepan.
4. Continue to whisk and remove from heat as soon as the butter begins to brown and gives off a nutty aroma.
5. Immediately transfer the butter to a medium sized bowl to prevent burning. Set aside and let it sit till cool to the touch.
6. In a mixing bowl, add cooled butter, sugars, eggs, vanilla, sour cream and baking soda. Beat till smooth. (1.5 c dark brown

sugar, ¼ c granulated sugar, 1 large egg, 1 tbs vanilla extract, 1 tbsp sour cream, 1 tsp baking soda)

7. Add in flour, till combined and fold in chocolate chips. Add pecans or walnuts, if desired. (2.25 c all purpose-flour, 1 c semi-sweet chocolate chips, 1 c milk chocolate chips, ½ c toasted pecans or walnuts)
8. Roll into 1 ½ in balls, place on a cookie sheet and freeze for 2 hours.
9. Pre-heat oven to 375 degrees. Bake for 9-11 minutes. Don't over bake. Bake till edges begin to brown.
10. Remove from oven, transfer cookies onto a cooling rack and let cool for about 10 minutes.

Red Velvet Chess Bars

Ingredients

- 1 box red velvet cake mix *(or any flavor mix you prefer)*
- 2 eggs, separated
- 2 sticks unsalted butter, melted and separated
- 8 oz cream cheese, softened
- 1 c powdered sugar
- 1 tsp vanilla

Directions

1. Preheat oven to 350 degrees.
2. Lightly spray 9x13 baking dish with nonstick cooking spray.
3. In a large bowl, combine cake mix, 1 egg, 1 stick of melted butter
4. Mix well until a dough forms.
5. Pour mixture into the baking dish, it will resemble dough.
6. Press the dough evenly into the prepared baking dish, spreading it to the edges with your hands.
7. In a separate bowl, combine remaining ingredients to make the filling.
8. Once combined, pour the filling over the top of of the dough and spread evenly.
9. Bake for 25-30 minutes. The middle will be slightly jiggly
10. Let the cake cool completely.
11. Cut into squares, then cover and chill before serving.

Peanut Butter Cookies

Ingredients

- 1 ½ c all-purpose flour
- ½ c unsalted butter, at room temperature
- 1 c peanut butter
- ½ c lightly packed brown sugar
- ½ c sugar
- 1 tsp vanilla extract
- 1 large egg, room temperature
- ¾ tsp baking powder

Directions

1. Preheat oven to 350F.
2. In a medium bowl, sift flour and baking powder, then whisk to combine.
3. In a stand mixer fitted with the paddle attachment, cream the butter and sugars. *If desired, add ¼–½ tsp of sea salt.*
4. Add the peanut butter and mix until fully incorporated.
5. Beat in the egg and vanilla extract, then add the flour mixture and mix until combined.
6. Roll dough into 1-inch balls and place them on a parchment lined baking sheet.
7. Flatten each cookie with a fork, creating a crisscross pattern.
8. Bake for about 10 minutes, or until the edges are lightly golden.
9. Allow the cookies to cool completely on the baking sheet before transferring--they need time to set.

Molasses Cookies

Ingredients

- ¾ c unsalted butter
- ½ c molasses
- 1 c brown sugar
- 1 egg
- 1 tsp cinnamon
- ¼ tsp nutmeg
- 2 tsp ginger
- ½ tsp salt
- 1 tsp baking soda
- 2¾ c all-purpose flour
- ½ c sugar *(for rolling the cookies)*

Directions

1. Preheat oven to 350 degrees.
2. In a large mixing bowl, cream butter and brown sugar together with a mixer.
3. Add the egg and molasses. Set aside.
4. In a separate bowl, whisk together the dry ingredients, *except the ½ cup sugar for rolling.*
5. Slowly add the dry ingredients to the wet mixture, until all ingredients are fully incorporated.
6. Form the dough into 2-inch balls, then coat each ball in the reserved sugar. Place on a parchment-lined baking sheet.
7. Bake for about 9 minutes.
8. Allow cookies to cool slightly on the baking sheet, then transfer to a baking rack to cool completely and set.

No-Bake Peanut Butter Cookies

Ingredients

- ½ c evaporated milk
- 1¾ c sugar
- ½ c *(1 stick)* salted butter, softened
- 1 tsp vanilla extract
- ¾ c creamy peanut butter
- 3 c quick oats *(do not use old-fashioned oats)*

Directions

1. In a heavy saucepan, combine the milk, sugar, and butter. Cook over medium heat, stirring constantly, until the mixture comes to a boil.
2. Once boiling, continue to cook and stir for one minute.
3. Remove from heat. Add the peanut butter, vanilla, and oats.
4. Stir quickly to combine, then drop the cookie mixture by spoonfuls onto wax paper to set.
5. Allow the cookies to cool completely, then store in an airtight container.

Fudgy Brownies

Ingredients

- 10 Tbs unsalted butter
- 1 ¼ c granulated sugar
- ¾ c plus 2 Tbs unsweetened cocoa powder
- 1 tsp vanilla extract
- ¼ tsp fine sea salt
- 2 large eggs, cold
- ½ c all-purpose flour, spooned and leveled
- ⅔ c chopped walnuts, pecans or chocolate chips *(optional)*

Directions

1. Position an oven rack in the center of the oven and preheat to 325°F.
2. Line the bottom and sides of an 8-inch square baking pan with parchment paper or aluminum foil, leaving an overhang on opposite sides to help lift the brownies out after baking.
3. Add the butter to a medium saucepan and place over medium-low heat. Cook until the butter is fully melted, then turn off the heat. Stay close and do not let it brown.
4. While the butter is still hot, stir in the sugar, cocoa powder, vanilla, and salt. Mix well until combined. *Don't worry if the batter looks gritty--it will smooth out once the eggs are added.*
5. Set the saucepan aside to cool until the mixture is warm, not hot (5 - 10 minutes). Test the temperature by touching the batter, it should be comfortable to hold without feeling hot.
6. Add the cold eggs, one at a time, stirring vigorously after each addition.

7. When the batter looks thick and well blended, add the flour. Use a wooden spoon or spatula to beat the flour into the batter until it becomes very thick and begins to pull away from the sides of the bowl. *I usually beat it for 40 to 50 strokes--see video for reference.*
8. Stir in nuts or chocolate chips, *optional.*
9. Spread the brownie batter evenly in the prepared pan. The batter will be quite thick, so do your best to push the batter to the corners and even out the top.
10. Bake for 20-30 minutes, or until the edges look dry and the center is slightly underbaked. A toothpick inserted into the center should emerge moist with batter. The brownies will continue to set as they cool but will stay moist and fudgy in the middle.
11. Allow the brownies to cool completely before removing them from the pan. *This step is essential for them to set properly.*
12. Cut into 16 squares. For clean edges, use a chef's knife and wipe it clean after each slice. For guaranteed perfect edges, chill the brownies in the fridge for 1-2 hours before slicing.

No Bake Cookies

Ingredients

- 2 c sugar
- ½ c whole milk
- ¼ c cocoa powder
- ¾ stick unsalted butter, softened
- ¾ c peanut butter
- 1 tsp vanilla extract
- 2-3 c quick oats

Directions

1. In a heavy saucepan over medium heat, combine the sugar, milk, cocoa powder and butter. *2 c sugar; ½ c whole milk; ¼ c cocoa powder; ¾ stick unsalted butter, softened*
2. Cook and stir constantly until the mixture comes to a full boil. Allow it to boil for about 1 minute, stirring continuously.
3. Remove the saucepan from heat.
4. Add the peanut butter and vanilla extract, stirring until smooth and well combined. *¾ c peanut butter, 1 tsp vanilla extract*
5. Stir in about 2 cups of oats.
6. Gradually add more oats, a little at a time, until the mixture reaches your desired consistency.
7. Work quickly, as the mixture will begin to set as it cools. *2-3 c quick oats*
8. Drop by spoonfuls onto buttered waxed paper.
9. Let cool completely until firm and set.

Blondie Brown Butter Brownies

Ingredients

- 1 c *(2 sticks)* unsalted butter
- 2 c packed light brown sugar
- 2 large eggs
- 1 Tbsp vanilla extract
- ½ tsp salt
- 1¾ c all-purpose flour
- ½ tsp baking powder
- ¾ c white chocolate chips *(optional but recommended)*
- ¾ cup chopped pecans or walnuts

Directions

Brown the Butter

1. In a medium saucepan over medium heat, melt the butter. Continue cooking, swirling the pan occasionally, until the butter turns golden brown and develops a nutty aroma, about 5–7 minutes.
2. Remove from heat and let cool for 10–15 minutes.

Mix the Wet Ingredients

3. In a large bowl, combine the browned butter and brown sugar. Whisk until smooth and well blended.
4. Add the eggs one at a time, whisking well after each.
5. Stir in the vanilla extract and salt until fully incorporated.

Add Dry Ingredients

6. In a separate bowl, whisk together the flour and baking powder.
7. Gradually stir the dry ingredients into the wet mixture until just combined. *Do not overmix.*
8. Fold in the chocolate chips and nuts, if using.

Bake

9. Preheat oven to 350°F.
10. Line a 9x13-inch baking pan with parchment paper or grease it well.
11. Spread batter evenly into the pan.
12. Bake for 25–30 minutes, or until the top is golden and a toothpick inserted in the center comes out with a few moist crumbs.

Cool & Slice

13. Allow the blondies to cool completely in the pan before slicing.
14. For clean, neat edges, chill fin the fridge for 15–20 minutes before slicing.

Trash Cookies

Ingredients

- 1 c brown sugar
- ½ c granulated sugar
- 2¼ c self-rising flour
- 1 egg
- 1 tsp pure vanilla extract
- 1 c *(2 sticks)* unsalted butter, softened
- 1 c chopped dark chocolate chunks
- 1 c toffee bits
- 1 c chopped pretzels
- 1 c sweetened shredded coconut *(optional)*

Directions

Brown the Butter

1. In a skillet on medium heat, brown the butter.
2. Remove from heat and let cool for about 20 minutes.

Mix the Dough

3. Once cooled, add the browned butter, both sugars and the vanilla extract to a mixing bowl. Beat till creamy.
4. Add the egg and mix till combined.
5. Gradually add the flour, till well combined.
6. Fold in the dark chocolate chunks, toffee bits, pretzels, and coconut (if using).
7. Chill the dough for about 1 hour.

Bake the Cookies

8. Preheat oven to 375 degrees.
9. Scoop 1–2-inch balls of dough onto a greased baking sheet.
10. Bake for 8-12 minutes. For softer cookies bake around 8-10 minutes.
11. Cool on the baking sheet for about 10 minutes, then transfer to a wire rack to cool completely.
12. Store in an air-tight container.

Lemon Chess Bars

Ingredients

Crust

- 1 box lemon cake mix
- 2 eggs
- ½ c *(1 stick)* unsalted butter, softened

Filling

- 8 oz cream cheese, softened
- 2 eggs
- 1½ powdered sugar
- ¼ c fresh lemon juice

Directions

Prepare the Crust

1. Preheat oven to 350°F.
2. In a medium bowl, combine the cake mix, eggs, and butter. Mix well until fully blended.
3. Press evenly into the bottom of a buttered 9x13 baking pan.

Prepare the Filling

4. In a separate bowl, combine the cream cheese, eggs, powdered sugar, and lemon juice. Mix till well combined.
5. Pour evenly over the crust.

Bake and Finish

6. Bake for about 30 minutes, or until the edges are lightly brown and the center is set but still slightly jiggly.
7. Dust with powdered sugar.
8. Let cool completely, then cut into squares.
9. Serve chilled or at room temperature.

BREADS

Banana Bread

Ingredients

- 3 ripe bananas, mashed
- 1 Tbsp vanilla extract
- 1 egg
- ½ c mayonnaise
- ½ c sugar
- 1 tsp cinnamon
- 1½ c self-rising flour

Nut Topping

- ½ c oats
- ½ c chopped pecans
- 1 Tbsp cinnamon
- ½ stick unsalted butter, melted
- 2 Tbsp brown sugar

Directions

1. Preheat oven to 375°F.
2. In a large bowl, mix the first six ingredients until well combined.
3. Gently fold in the flour until incorporated — *do not overmix.*
4. Pour the batter into a greased 9x5-inch loaf pan.
5. In a small bowl, prepare the nut topping by combining all topping ingredients. Sprinkle evenly over the batter.
6. Bake for 35–45 minutes, or until a toothpick inserted into the center comes out clean. *Do not overbake.*
7. Allow the bread to cool slightly before slicing. Serve warm or at room temperature.

Cream Biscuits

(2 ingredients)

Ingredients

- 2 c self-rising flour
- 1½ c heavy whipping cream

Directions

1. Preheat oven to 400°F.
2. Lightly coat a baking sheet or cast-iron skillet with shortening and set aside.
3. In a large mixing bowl, add the flour. Gradually pour in the heavy cream, stirring gently until just combined. *Do not overmix.*
4. Turn the dough out onto a lightly floured surface. Gently pat or roll it to about ½ inch thickness.
5. Cut out biscuits using a 2-inch biscuit cutter. Do not twist the biscuit cutter, as this can prevent the biscuits from rising properly.
6. Place the biscuits on the prepared baking sheet, leaving about 1 inch of space between them to allow for even rising and thorough baking.
7. Bake for 10–12 minutes, or until golden brown.
8. Remove from the oven and serve warm.

These are the best biscuits with fruit jams, honey, cooked apples or honey butter.

Pumpkin Roll

Ingredients

Cake

- 3 eggs
- 1 c sugar
- ⅔ c pumpkin purée
- 1 tsp lemon juice
- ¾ c self-rising flour
- 2 tsp cinnamon
- 1 tsp ground ginger
- ½ tsp nutmeg

Filling

- 1 *(8 oz)* block cream cheese, softened
- 2 c powdered sugar
- 1 *(8 oz)* container whipped topping

Directions

Cake

1. Preheat oven to 350°F.
2. In a large bowl, mix all of the cake ingredients (except filling) together until well combined.
3. Line the bottom of a cookie sheet or jelly roll pan with parchment paper and lightly coat with nonstick spray.
4. Pour the batter onto the prepared pan and spread it evenly.
5. Bake for about 15 minutes.
6. Carefully flip the warm cake onto a cheesecloth that has been generously sprinkled with powdered sugar.
7. Gently roll the cake up in the towel and let it cool completely at room temperature.

Filling

8. For the filling, combine the cream cheese and powdered sugar in a bowl. Beat until creamy and smooth, then fold in the whipped topping.
9. Once the cake is cooled, unroll it carefully and spread the filling evenly over the surface, all the way to the edges.
10. Re-roll the cake, wrap it, and chill until firm.
11. Slice into even pieces.

Cinnamon Bread

Ingredients

- 2 c all-purpose flour
- 1 c white sugar
- 1 c buttermilk
- 2 large eggs
- ¼ c vegetable oil
- 2 tsp vanilla extract
- 2 tsp baking powder
- 1½ tsp ground cinnamon
- 1 tsp salt
- ½ tsp baking soda

Topping:

- 2 Tbsp white sugar
- 2 tsp salted butter
- 1 tsp ground cinnamon

Directions

1. Preheat oven to 350°F. Generously grease a 9x5-inch loaf pan.

Bread

2. In a large mixing bowl, beat together the flour, sugar, buttermilk, eggs, oil, vanilla, baking powder, cinnamon, salt, and baking soda until well combined, about 3 minutes.
3. Pour the batter into the prepared loaf pan and smooth the top.

Topping

4. In a small bowl, stir together the sugar, melted butter, and cinnamon until crumbly. Sprinkle evenly over the batter. Use a paring knife to gently swirl the batter for a marbled effect.

5. Bake in the preheated oven until a toothpick inserted into the center comes out clean, about 50 minutes.
6. Remove the bread from the pan and transfer to a wire rack to cool completely before slicing.

Hot Rolls (Yeast Rolls)

Ingredients

- 1 package instant dry yeast
- ¼ c warm water
- 3 Tbsp sugar
- ¾ c warm whole milk
- 3 Tbsp unsalted butter, melted
- 1¼ tsp salt
- 1 egg, beaten
- 2-3 c all-purpose flour *(plus more for kneading)*
- Additional melted salted butter *(for brushing the tops of the rolls)*

Directions

1. In a small bowl, combine the yeast, warm water, and sugar to activate the yeast. Stir to dissolve and let sit for about 5 minutes, or until the mixture becomes bubbly.
2. In a large mixing bowl, combine the warm milk, egg, yeast mixture, melted butter, and salt. Stir to blend.
3. Gradually add the flour, mixing until a sticky dough forms. Cover the bowl with a clean towel and let rise in a warm area until doubled in size, about 1 hour.
4. Punch down the dough and transfer it to a floured surface. Knead for about 5 minutes, adding small amounts of flour as needed until the dough is smooth and elastic.
5. Pinch off portions of dough and shape into 2-inch balls. Place them in a buttered metal baking pan, spacing slightly apart.
6. Cover and let rise again in a warm area until doubled in size, about 1 hour.

7. Preheat oven to 400°F. Brush the tops of the rolls with melted salted butter.
8. Bake for 10–15 minutes, or until the tops are golden brown.
9. Brush with additional melted butter just before serving.

This recipe makes about 18 rolls and can be doubled.

Country Corn Bread (Not Sweet)

Ingredients

- 3 c self-rising cornmeal mix
- 1¾ c buttermilk
- ½ stick butter, melted
- 2 large eggs
- ¼ c lard or shortening *(for greasing the skillet)*

Directions

1. Preheat oven to 400°F.
2. Grease a large cast-iron skillet (I use a 10 inch) with lard or shortening. Place the skillet in the oven to heat while you prepare the batter.
3. In a large mixing bowl, combine the cornmeal mix, buttermilk, melted butter, and eggs. Stir till well combined, but do not over stir.
4. Carefully remove the hot skillet from the oven. Sprinkle a small amount of dry cornmeal mix into the bottom of the skillet (a little secret to a crunchy crust).
5. Pour the batter into the hot skillet and return it to the oven.
6. Bake for 30–40 minutes, or until golden brown and firm in the center.

Cracklin' Corn Bread

Ingredients

- 2 c self-rising cornmeal mix
- 2 eggs
- ¼ c butter, melted
- 1 tsp black pepper
- Buttermilk *(enough to make a wet batter)*
- 2 c pork cracklings
- 3-4 Tbsp bacon grease *(for greasing the skillet.)*

Directions

1. Preheat oven to 400°F.
2. Add the bacon grease to a 9–10 inch cast-iron skillet and place it in the oven to heat.
3. In a large mixing bowl, combine the cornmeal mix, eggs, melted butter, and black pepper. Stir in enough buttermilk to create a thick, pancake-like batter.
4. Fold in the pork cracklings until evenly distributed.
5. Carefully remove the hot skillet from the oven and pour the batter into it.
6. Bake for 30–40 minutes, or until golden brown.

Sweet Onion Upside Down Cornbread

Ingredients

- 1 stick butter, melted.
- 3 large Vidalia onions, sliced ½ inch thick *(or enough to cover the bottom of the pan)*
- 3 c self-rising cornmeal mix
- 3 eggs, beaten.
- 2 c buttermilk
- 1½ c grated sharp cheddar cheese.
- 2 finely chopped jalapeños *(optional)*
- 2 Tbsp sugar *(optional, but enhances the sweet onion flavor)*

Directions

1. Preheat oven to 400°F.
2. In a 10-inch cast-iron skillet, add the melted butter and sliced onions. Bake for 10-15 minutes, or until the onions begin to soften and turn golden.
3. In a large bowl, combine the cornmeal mix, eggs, buttermilk, and sugar. Stir just till combined.
4. Fold in the cheese and jalapeños (if using).
5. Carefully remove the skillet from the oven and pour the batter evenly over the onions.
6. Return to the oven and bake for 35–45 minutes, or until golden brown and fully set in the center.

7. Loosen the edges with a knife, and invert the cornbread onto a plate.
8. Allow to cool slightly before cutting into squares and serving warm.

Buttery Layered Square Biscuits

Ingredients

- 1½ c self-rising flour
- ¾ cup frozen unsalted butter
- ½ - ¾ c buttermilk or whole milk
- 1 heaping tsp baking powder
- Melted salted butter *(for brushing the tops)*

Directions

1. Preheat oven to 425°F.
2. In a large mixing bowl, combine the flour and baking powder. Stir to blend.
3. Using a cheese grater, grate the frozen butter directly into the flour. Toss gently until the butter is evenly distributed.
4. Gradually stir in the buttermilk, a little at a time, just until a sticky, wet dough forms.
5. Lightly flour your hands or a rolling pin, then shape the dough into a rectangle, working from the center outward. *Avoid pressing too hard—aim for about ½-inch thickness.*
6. Fold one-third of the rectangle over toward the center, and repeat the other side. Flip the dough so the seams are underneath. This time fold the dough over in half (not in thirds) and roll into another rectangle. Repeat all the folds again (you're creating layers).
7. Now cut the biscuits with a pizza cutter or sharp knife into six even sized squares. Place on a buttered baking sheet.

8. Place the biscuits on a buttered baking sheet, spacing them about 2 inches apart.
9. Bake for about 8 minutes or until golden brown.
10. Brush the hot biscuits generously with melted salted butter before serving.

Buttermilk Cathead Biscuits

Ingredients

- 2 c self-rising flour
- ⅓ c lard
- ¾ c buttermilk *(may need 1 cup, enough to make a sticky dough)*
- Salted butter or bacon grease *(for Basting)*
- Butter *(for greasing the pan, cast-iron skillet, or griddle)*

Directions

1. Preheat oven to 400°F.
2. Place the flour in a large mixing bowl. Add the lard and use your hands or a fork to cut it into the flour until the mixture is crumbly and resembles cornmeal.
   (2 c self-rising flour, one-third c lard)
3. Gradually stir in the buttermilk until a sticky dough forms. It should be moist but not overly wet. (¾ c buttermilk)
4. Lightly sprinkle flour over the dough and flour your hands to prevent sticking. (2 c self-rising flour)
5. Pinch up enough dough to form a 2-inch ball. Gently roll it between your hands, tucking the seam underneath and smoothing the top. *Be careful not to overwork the dough.*
6. Place the biscuits in a buttered baking dish or cast-iron skillet, letting them touch slightly. (I use a cast-iron griddle or skillet.)

7. Brush the tops with melted salted butter or bacon grease — *just like Mamaw did.*
8. Bake for 20-25 minutes, or till golden brown.
9. Remove from oven and brush again with melted butter or bacon grease before serving warm.

Kenzie's Sourdough Bread

Ingredients:

- 1 c active, bubbly starter
- 1 c warm water
- 3 c bread flour
- 1 tsp salt

Directions

Prepare Ingredients

1. In a large bowl, combine the active starter and warm water, mixing until fully combined.
2. Add the flour and salt, then mix with your hands until a shaggy dough forms. The dough may feel slightly dry at this stage — add up to ¼ cup of warm water, a little at a time, until the dough is tacky but not runny.
3. Once ingredients are mixed well, cover the bowl with a tea towel and let the dough rest for 1 hour.

Stretch and Fold (4 Sets)

4. After an hour, complete 4 sets of stretch and folds:
5. Keeping the dough in the bowl, gently lift one corner of the dough, stretch it upward without tearing, and fold it back toward the center.
6. Repeat on all four sides.
7. Repeat this stretch-and-fold process every 30 minutes for a total of 4 sets.
8. After the fourth set, cover the dough again and let it rest at room temperature for 2 hours.

Shape the Dough

9. After 2 hours, pour the dough onto a lightly floured surface.
10. Gently flatten the dough into a large square, being careful not to press too thin or tear the dough. The dough should not tear.
11. Fold in each side to make a skinny rectangle.
12. Then, roll from the bottom up to shape it into a ball.

Proofing

13. Place the dough, seam-side up, into a bowl lined with a floured tea towel. Cover and refrigerate for 2–3 hours to proof. *This step develops the sour flavor — don't skip it!*

Baking

14. After proofing, preheat the oven to 450°F. Place your Dutch oven inside to heat while the oven preheats.
15. Once the oven is hot, plop the dough onto a piece of parchment paper and lightly coat the top with flour. Score the top of the dough, then carefully place it (with the parchment paper) into the preheated Dutch oven.
16. Bake for 30 minutes with the lid on, then remove the lid and bake for an additional 20–25 minutes, or until golden brown.
17. Transfer the loaf to a cooling rack and let cool for at least 1 hour before slicing.

Pone Bread (Biscuit Bread)

Ingredients

- 2 c self-rising flour
- ¼ c melted lard, shortening or butter *(plus a little extra for greasing the skillet)*
- 1½ c buttermilk
- Melted salted butter *(for brushing on after baking)*

Directions

1. Preheat oven to 375°F.
2. Grease an 8- or 9-inch cast-iron skillet with lard, shortening or butter. (¼ c melted lard, shortening or butter)

   Tip: Place the skillet in the oven while it heats. This helps create a crust.
3. In a large mixing bowl, combine the flour, melted lard, and buttermilk. Stir until just combined; the batter should resemble a thick pancake batter. *Do not overmix.* (2 c self-rising flour, ¼ c melted lard, shortening or butter, 1½ c buttermilk)
4. Carefully pour the batter into the hot skillet and spread evenly.
5. Bake for about 30 minutes, or till golden brown.
6. Remove from the oven and brush the top generously with melted salted butter. Serve warm. (melted salted butter)

Garlic Cheddar Biscuits

Ingredients

- 2½ c self-rising flour
- ¼ c cold unsalted butter
- ¾ c buttermilk *(may need more)*
- ½ tsp garlic powder
- 1 c shredded sharp cheddar cheese

Topping

- ¼ c melted salted butter
- ¼ tsp garlic powder
- ½ tsp parsley

Directions

1. Preheat oven to 400°F.
2. Combine flour and butter. Cut butter into the flour till pea sized. (2½ c self-rising flour, ¼ c cold unsalted butter)
3. Mix in cheese and garlic powder. (1 c shredded sharp cheddar cheese, ¼ tsp garlic powder)
4. Add enough buttermilk to make a sticky dough. (¾ c buttermilk)
5. Sprinkle some flour on the dough and flour your hands. (2½ c self-rising flour)
6. Pinch up enough dough and gently form into 2-inch round biscuits. Tuck the seams with your thumbs, but don't overwork the dough.
7. Place biscuits on a buttered baking dish or skillet.
8. Bake for 20-25 min, or till browned.
9. While the biscuits bake, prepare the topping by combining the melted butter, garlic powder, and parsley.

10. Remove the biscuirts from the oven and immediately brush with the garlic butter mixture. Serve warm. (½ tsp garlic powder, ½ tsp parsley, ¼ c melted salted butter)

Homemade Sandwich Bread

Ingredients

- 2 c warm water *(no hotter than 115°F — higher heat can kill the yeast and the bread will not rise properly)*
- 1 Tbsp active dry yeast
- ¼ c honey *(or sugar-free syrup of your choice)*
- 2 Tbsp avocado oil
- 2 tsp salt
- 5 c bread flour *(all-purpose, may be substituted, but bread flour is better)*
- Additional flour *(for dusting)*

Directions

1. In a large mixing bowl, combine the warm water and yeast. Stir gently and let the mixture proof for about 5 minutes, or until bubbly and fragrant.
2. Add the honey, avocado oil, salt, and flour. Mix with a dough hook or by hand until the dough comes together and begins to pull away from the sides of the bowl.
3. Cover the bowl with a clean towel and let the dough rise in a warm place for about 1 hour.
4. Punch down the dough and transfer it to a lightly floured surface. Knead for about 5 minutes, then divide it into two equal pieces.
5. Roll each piece into a rectangle, then roll it up tightly into a loaf shape. Place each loaf seam-side down into a parchment-lined loaf pan.

6. Cover and let rise again for about 1 hour, or until the dough has doubled in size.
7. Brush the top with melted salted butter.
8. Bake in a preheated 375°F oven for about 1 hour, or until golden brown and cooked through in the center.
9. Remove from the oven, brush again with melted butter if desired, and cool on a wire rack before slicing.

Cinnamon Rolls

Ingredients

- 1 recipe for hot rolls
- Ground cinnamon *(to taste)*
- 1 stick butter, melted
- 2 c brown sugar
- 1 c chopped pecans *(optional)*

Directions

1. Prepare the dough using my Hot Roll recipe, but skip the step where you shape the dough into balls.
2. On a lightly floured surface, roll the dough into a large rectangle about ¼ inch thick.
3. Pour the melted butter over the dough and spread evenly with your hands.
4. Sprinkle the brown sugar evenly over the surface, then generously dust with ground cinnamon. Add the chopped pecans, if desired.
5. Starting from the long edge farthest from you, roll the dough tightly toward yourself. When you reach the end, pinch the seam closed and place the roll seam-side down.
6. Slice the roll into ½-inch-thick pieces. *I use thread or unflavored dental floss.*
7. Arrange the rolls in a buttered baking dish, spacing them slightly apart. *Do not overcrowd the pan* — about 7–9 rolls per pan works best.
8. Cover with a towel and let rise in a warm spot until doubled in size.

9. Bake in a preheated 375°F oven for 15–20 minutes, or until golden brown.
10. While still warm, top with my Cream Cheese Frosting recipe, covering all the way to the edges.
11. Let cool slightly before serving.

LOW CARB/LOW SUGAR SWEETS

Low-Carb Fudgy Brownies

Ingredients

- ½ c *(1 stick)* unsalted butter
- ½ c unsweetened cocoa powder
- ⅔ c granulated erythritol *(or monk fruit/stevia blend)*
- 2 large eggs
- 1 tsp vanilla extract
- ¼ c almond flour
- ¼ tsp salt
- ¼ tsp baking powder *(optional, for slightly cakier texture)*
- ¼ c sugar-free chocolate chips

Directions

1. Preheat oven to 350°F. Line an 8x8-inch baking pan with parchment paper or grease well.
2. In a medium saucepan over low heat, melt the butter. Once melted, remove from heat and whisk in the cocoa powder and erythritol until smooth.
3. Let the mixture cool slightly, then whisk in the eggs one at a time. Stir in the vanilla extract.
4. Add the almond flour, salt, and baking powder (if using). Mix just until combined—*do not overmix*.
5. Fold in the sugar-free chocolate chips, if using.
6. Pour the batter into the prepared pan and spread evenly.

7. Bake for 18–22 minutes, or until the top is set and a toothpick inserted into the center comes out with moist crumbs (not wet batter).
8. Allow the brownies to cool completely in the pan before cutting. They will firm up as they cool.

Low Carb Pound Cake

Ingredients

- 1½ c almond flour *(super-fine works best)*
- ¼ c coconut flour
- 1 tsp baking powder
- ¼ tsp salt
- ½ c *(1 stick)* unsalted butter, softened
- ¾ c erythritol or other keto-friendly sweetener *(like allulose or monk fruit)*
- 4 large eggs, room temperature
- 1 tsp vanilla extract
- ½ tsp almond extract *(optional)*
- ¼ c heavy cream

Directions

1. Preheat your oven to 350°F. Grease a loaf pan and line it with parchment paper.
2. In a medium bowl, whisk together the almond flour, coconut flour, baking powder, and salt
3. In a large bowl, cream the butter and sweetener together till light and fluffy.
4. Beat in the eggs one at a time, ensuring each is fully incorporated before adding the next.
5. Mix in the vanilla extract, almond extract (if using), and heavy cream.
6. Gradually add the dry ingredients to the wet mixture, stirring till just combined. *Do not overmix.*

7. Pour the batter into the prepared loaf pan and smooth the top evenly.
8. Bake for 45–55 minutes, or till a toothpick inserted into the center comes out clean. *If the top begins to brown too quickly, cover loosely with foil around the 35-minute mark.*
9. Let the loaf cool in the pan for 10 minutes, then transfer to a wire rack to cool completely before slicing.

Carb Chocolate Fudge

Ingredients

- 1 c sugar-free chocolate chips
- ½ c heavy cream
- ¼ c unsalted butter
- ¼ c powdered erythritol or allulose *(adjust to taste)*
- 1 tsp vanilla extract
- Pinch of salt
- Optional: ¼ c chopped nuts *(pecans or walnuts)* or unsweetened shredded coconut

Directions

1. **Prepare the Pan**
   Line a small square pan (such as an 8x4-inch loaf pan or 6x6-inch pan) with parchment paper, leaving some overhang for easy removal.
2. **Melt the Base**
   In a medium saucepan over medium-low heat, combine the chocolate chips, butter, and heavy cream. Stir constantly till the mixture is fully melted and smooth.
3. **Sweeten & Flavor**
   Remove from heat and stir in the powdered erythritol, vanilla extract, and salt. Taste and adjust sweetness if desired. If using, fold in the nuts or shredded coconut.
4. **Chill**
   Pour the mixture into the prepared pan and smooth the top evenly. Chill in the refrigerator for at least 2 hours, or till firm.

5. **Slice & Serve**

Once set, lift the fudge from the pan using the parchment paper and cut into small squares. Store in the refrigerator till ready to serve.

Low-Carb Cheesecake

Ingredients

Crust

- 1½ c almond flour
- ¼ c melted butter
- 2 Tbsp erythritol or monk fruit sweetener
- ½ tsp vanilla extract

Filling

- 24 oz *(3 blocks)* cream cheese, softened
- ¾ c powdered keto sweetener
- 3 large eggs
- 1 tsp vanilla extract
- ¼ c sour cream
- 1 Tbsp lemon juice

Directions

Make the Crust

1. Preheat oven to 325°F.
2. In a medium bowl, combine the almond flour, melted butter, sweetener, and vanilla extract. Mix till the mixture resembles coarse crumbs.
3. Press evenly into the bottom of a 9-inch springform pan.
4. Bake for 10–12 minutes, or till lightly golden.
5. Remove from the oven and let cool completely.

Prepare the Filling

6. In a large mixing bowl, beat the cream cheese and powdered sweetener together till smooth and creamy.

7. Add the eggs one at a time, mixing well after each addition.
8. Stir in the vanilla extract, sour cream, and lemon juice till fully combined, smooth, and creamy.

Assemble & Bake

9. Pour the filling over the cooled crust.
10. Bake at 325°F for 50–60 minutes, or till the edges are set but the center still jiggles slightly.

Cool & Chill

11. Turn off the oven, crack the door open slightly, and let the cheesecake cool in the oven for 1 hour.
12. Transfer to the refrigerator and chill for at least 4 hours, or overnight for best results.

Cool & Chill

13. Remove from the springform pan, slice, and serve chilled.

Low Carb Peanut Butter Pie

Ingredients

Crust

- 1½ c almond flour
- 3 Tbsp melted butter
- 2 Tbsp powdered erythritol *(Swerve or monk fruit)*
- ½ tsp vanilla extract
- Pinch of salt

Filling

- 1 c natural peanut butter *(smooth, no sugar added)*
- 8 oz cream cheese, softened
- ¾ c powdered erythritol
- 1 tsp vanilla extract
- 1 c heavy whipping cream *(whipped to stiff peaks)*

Directions

Make the Crust

1. Preheat oven to 350°F.
2. In a medium bowl, combine the almond flour, melted butter, sweetener, vanilla extract, and salt. Mix till a crumbly dough forms.
3. Press the mixture evenly into a 9-inch pie dish.
4. Bake for 8–10 minutes, or till lightly golden. Remove from the oven and let cool completely.

Prepare the Filling

5. In a large mixing bowl, beat together the cream cheese and peanut butter till smooth and creamy.
6. Add the powdered sweetener and vanilla extract, mixing till fully incorporated.
7. Gently fold in the whipped cream till the mixture is light and fluffy.

Assemble

8. Pour the filling into the cooled crust and smooth the top with a spatula.
9. Refrigerate for at least 3 hours, or till set. For best results, chill overnight before serving.

Low-Carb Chocolate Chip Cookies

Ingredients

- 1½ c almond flour
- ¼ c softened butter *(or coconut oil for dairy-free)*
- ⅓ c powdered keto sweetener
- 1 large egg
- ½ tsp vanilla extract
- ¼ tsp baking soda
- ¼ tsp salt
- ½ c sugar-free chocolate chips

Directions

1. Preheat oven to 350°F. Line a baking sheet with parchment paper.
2. In a medium bowl, cream together the butter and sweetener till smooth.
3. Add the egg and vanilla extract, mixing till fully combined.
4. Stir in the almond flour, baking soda, and salt till a soft dough forms.
5. Fold in the chocolate chips
6. Scoop the dough onto the prepared baking sheet using a tablespoon or small cookie scoop.
7. Flatten each cookie slightly with the back of a spoon — they won't spread much while baking.
8. Bake for 10–12 minutes, or till the edges are lightly golden.

9. Let cool on the baking sheet for 10 minutes before transferring to a wire rack.

Low Carb Peanut Butter Fudge

Ingredients

- 1 c natural peanut butter *(smooth, unsweetened, no added sugar)*
- ½ c coconut oil *(or unsalted butter, melted)*
- ⅓ c powdered monk fruit sweetener
- 1 tsp vanilla extract
- Pinch of salt *(optional, if peanut butter is unsalted)*

Directions

Melt Ingredients

1. In a medium saucepan over low heat, melt the peanut butter and coconut oil together, stirring constantly to avoid scorching, until smooth. Be careful not to let the mixture scorch.

Add Sweetener & Extract

2. Remove from heat. Stir in the monk fruit sweeter/powdered erythritol, vanilla extract, and salt (if using). Mix until fully combined and smooth.

Pour & Chill

3. Line an 8x8-inch pan (or a loaf pan for thicker pieces) with parchment paper. Pour the mixture into the prepared pan and smooth the top evenly.
4. Pour the mixture into the pan and smooth the top evenly.

Refrigerate

5. Chill in the fridge for at least 1–2 hours, or until firm.
6. Cut into squares & store in an airtight container in the refrigerator.

Cakes/Pies/ Frostings

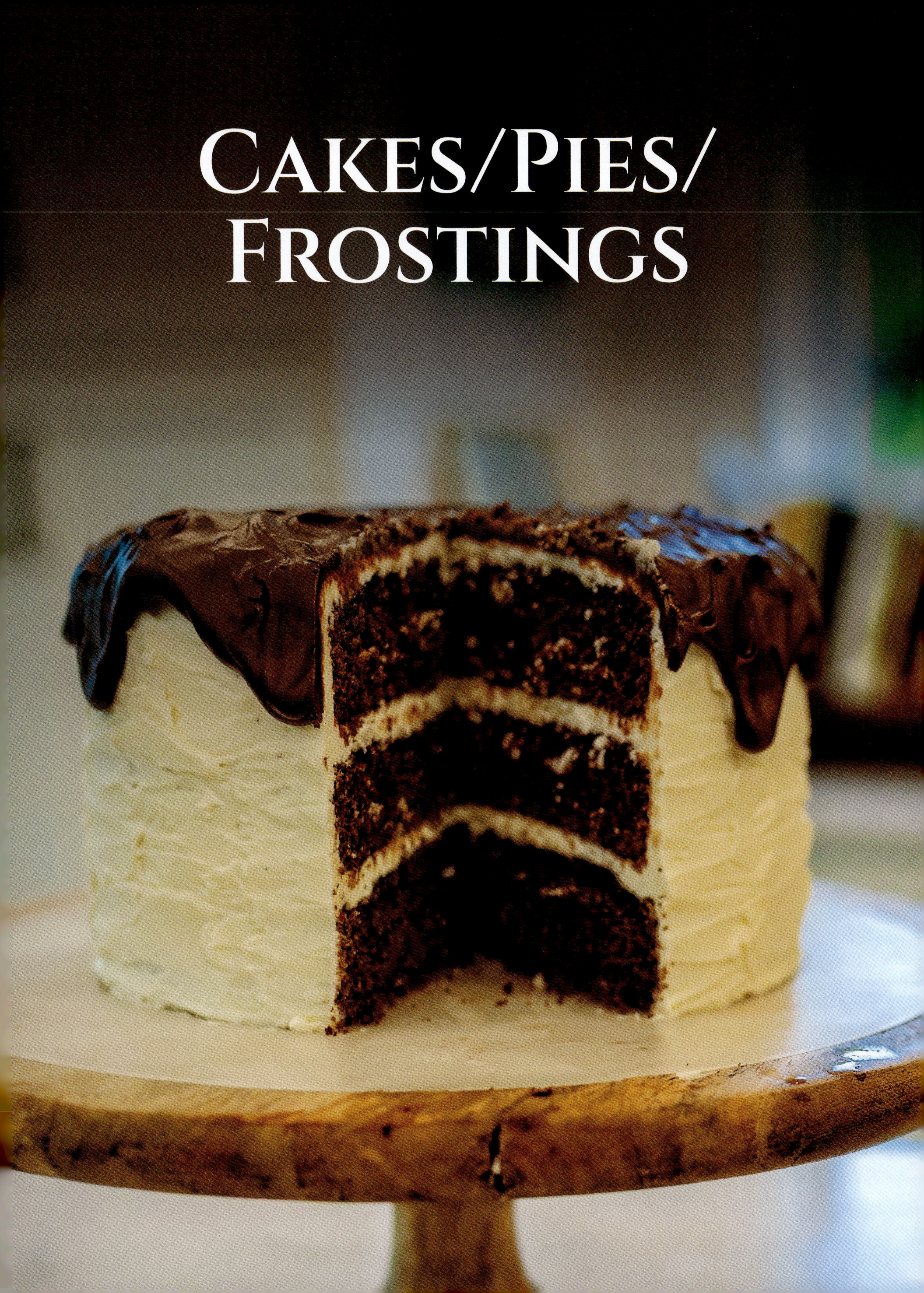

Vanilla Buttercream Frosting

Ingredients

- 3 sticks unsalted butter, room temperature
- 6 c powdered sugar
- ⅓ c heavy cream, room temperature
- 3 tsp pure vanilla extract
- 1/8 tsp salt *(optional, helps to cut sweetness)*

Directions

1. In a large bowl, using a hand or stand mixer fitted with the paddle attachment, beat the butter on medium till creamy, about 2 minutes.
2. Reduce the mixer speed to low and gradually add the powdered sugar, heavy cream, vanilla extract, and salt. Mix till combined.
3. Increase to high speed and beat for about 3 minutes, or till the frosting is light, fluffy, and smooth.
4. If the frosting is too thin, add more powdered sugar a little at a time. If too thick, mix in a small splash of cream. If too sweet, add a pinch more salt.
5. Yield: Enough to frost a 2- to 3-layer cake.

Tip: *For chocolate buttercream, add ½ cup unsweetened cocoa powder to the sugar.*

Cream Cheese Frosting

Ingredients

- 2 c 8oz blocks cream cheese, room temperature
- 1 c unsalted butter, softened
- 4-6 c powdered sugar
- 2 tsp vanilla extract

Directions

1. In a large mixing bowl, beat the cream cheese and butter together till smooth and fluffy, about 2–3 minutes.
2. Gradually add the powdered sugar and vanilla extract.
3. Continue beating on medium-high speed for 2–3 minutes, or till light and creamy.

Recipe Note

This recipe makes enough frosting for a three-layer, 8- or 9-inch cake. For smaller cakes, the recipe can be halved.

Vanilla Ermine Frosting (Boiled Milk Frosting)

Ingredients

- 1½ c whole milk
- 7 Tbsp all-purpose flour
- 1½ c granulated sugar
- 2 tsp vanilla extract
- ½ tsp salt
- 1½ c *(3 sticks)* unsalted butter, room temperature

Directions

1. In a medium saucepan, combine the sugar, flour, and salt. Whisk well to combine and remove any lumps.
2. Place the pan over medium heat and gradually whisk in the milk till the mixture is smooth.
3. Continue whisking constantly till the mixture thickens to a pudding-like consistency. *Do not increase the heat, as the mixture will burn and the sugar will not dissolve properly.*
4. Remove the pan from the heat and pour the mixture into a heatproof bowl.
5. Press a piece of plastic wrap directly onto the surface of the mixture to prevent a skin from forming as it cools.
6. Allow the mixture to cool completely to room temperature.
7. In a large mixing bowl, using a stand or hand mixer, beat the butter till light and fluffy. Scrape down the sides of the bowl occasionally.

8. Reduce the mixer speed and add the cooled flour mixture one spoonful at a time, ensuring each addition is fully incorporated before adding the next.
9. Scrape down the sides of the bowl periodically with a spatula to ensure even mixing.
10. Add the vanilla extract and continue mixing till well combined.
11. Once all of the flour mixture has been added, increase the mixer speed to medium-high and whip till the frosting is smooth, light, and fluffy.
12. *(Optional)* To make chocolate frosting, add ¼ cup of cocoa powder to the whipped butter when adding the flour mixture.

This is the original, less-sweet frosting for red velvet cake, but it can be used with any type of cake.

Red Velvet Cake

Ingredients

- 2½ c all-purpose flour
- 1½ c sugar
- 1 tsp salt
- 1 heaping tsp cocoa powder
- 1 c buttermilk, room temperature
- 1½ c canola oil
- 2 eggs, room temperature
- 1 tsp vanilla extract
- 1 *(1-ounce)* bottle red food coloring
- 1 tsp vinegar
- 1 tsp baking soda
- Chopped pecans *(for garnish, optional)*

Directions

1. Preheat the oven to 325°F.
2. Grease and flour three 9-inch cake pans.
3. Sift together the flour, salt, sugar, and cocoa powder.
4. Add the buttermilk, food coloring, oil, eggs, and vanilla to the dry ingredients. Mix well, but do not overmix.
5. In a small bowl, combine the vinegar and baking soda. Add this mixture to the batter, folding it in gently.
6. Divide the batter evenly among the prepared pans and tap them lightly on the counter to remove air bubbles.
7. Bake for 30–35 minutes, or till a toothpick inserted in the center comes out clean. Do not overbake.
8. Cool cakes completely before frosting. Frost with cream cheese or ermine frosting and garnish with chopped pecans.

Classic Carrot Cake

Ingredients

- 2 c sugar
- 1½ c vegetable oil
- 4 eggs, room temperature
- 1 tsp vanilla extract
- 1 heaping tsp cinnamon
- ¼ heaping tsp baking soda
- ¼ heaping tsp baking powder
- ¼ tsp salt
- 2 c all-purpose flour
- 2 c finely shredded fresh carrots
- Pecan halves, for garnish

Directions

1. Preheat oven to 350°F.
2. In a large mixing bowl, combine the oil, sugar, eggs, and vanilla. Mix till smooth.
3. In a separate bowl, whisk together the flour, cinnamon, salt, baking soda, and baking powder.
4. Gradually add the dry ingredients to the wet mixture, stirring till just combined. *Do not overmix.*
5. Fold in the shredded carrots till evenly combined
6. Divide the batter evenly between two greased or nonstick-sprayed 8-inch round cake pans.
7. Bake for 30–40 minutes, or till a toothpick inserted into the center comes out clean. *Avoid overbaking.*
8. Let the cakes cool completely in the pans before removing.
9. Frost with cream cheese frosting (see recipe) and garnish with pecan halves.

Cake can be baked in a 9x13 pan also.

Black Walnut Cake

Ingredients

- 2 c sifted all-purpose flour
- 2 tsp baking powder
- ½ tsp salt
- ½ tsp baking soda
- 1 tsp vanilla extract
- 1½ c sugar
- ⅔ c vegetable shortening
- ¾ c buttermilk
- 3 eggs, separated
- 2 c black walnuts *(toss in a little flour to prevent sinking while baking)*
- 1 recipe for Cream Cheese Frosting *(Page 67)*

Directions

1. Preheat oven to 350°F.
2. In a large bowl, beat the egg whites till stiff peaks form. Set aside.
3. In a separate mixing bowl, cream together the shortening, sugar, and vanilla till light and fluffy.
4. Add the egg yolks one at a time, beating well after each addition.
5. In a medium bowl, whisk together the sifted dry ingredients.
6. Add the dry ingredients and buttermilk alternately to the creamed mixture in small amounts, mixing well after each addition.
7. Add the black walnuts, then gently fold in the stiffly beaten egg whites till combined.
8. Grease and flour a Bundt pan. Pour the batter evenly into the pan.

9. Bake for 25–30 minutes, or till a toothpick inserted in the center comes out clean.
10. Let the cake cool in the pan for about 10 minutes, then transfer to a wire rack to cool completely.
11. Once cooled, frost with cream cheese frosting.

Coal Miners Cake

Ingredients

Cake:

- 1 box devil's food cake mix
- 1 *(20 oz)* can cherry pie filling
- 2 eggs
- 1 tsp vanilla

Icing:

- 1 c sugar
- 1 stick unsalted butter, room temperature
- ¼ c evaporated milk
- 6 oz chocolate chips
- ½ c chopped pecans

Directions

Prepare the Cake

1. Preheat oven to 350°F.
2. In a large bowl, combine the cake mix, cherry pie filling, eggs, and vanilla. Mix till just combined—do not overmix.
3. Pour the batter into a greased 9x13-inch baking pan and bake for 30–35 minutes, or till a toothpick inserted in the center comes out clean.
4. Do not overbake.

Make the Icing

5. In a saucepan over low heat, combine the sugar, butter, and evaporated milk.
6. Bring to a low boil and cook for 1 minute.

7. Remove from heat and stir in the chocolate chips and pecans till smooth.

Assemble and Serve

8. Pour the warm icing over the cake while it's still hot.
9. Serve warm, chilled or at room temperature.

Mamaw's Apple Butter Stack Cake (Easy Version)

Ingredients

- ¾ c Unsalted butter
- ½ c sugar
- 2 eggs
- 1 c molasses
- ¼ tsp baking soda
- ½ c buttermilk
- ¼ tsp salt
- ¼ tsp cloves
- ¾ tsp allspice
- ¾ tsp cinnamon
- 3 c all-purpose flour
- 1 tsp baking powder

Directions

1. Cream the butter and sugar together in a large mixing bowl till light and fluffy.
2. Add the eggs and molasses, mixing well to combine.
3. In a small bowl, stir the baking soda into the buttermilk and set aside.
4. In a separate bowl, whisk together all the dry ingredients.
5. Add the dry ingredients to the butter mixture alternately with the buttermilk, beginning and ending with the dry ingredients.
6. Divide the batter evenly among six 9-inch cake pans, spreading each layer about ½ inch thick. Spray the pans with nonstick cooking spray.
7. Bake at 350°F for about 12 minutes.
8. Let the cake layers cool completely before assembling.

Filling

3 Cups apple butter or apple sauce

9. Spread the apple butter (or applesauce) between the cooled cake layers and over the entire outside of the cake.
10. Cover and refrigerate overnight. Serve chilled or at room temperature.

Note: *This recipe can be doubled for a taller cake.*

Old Timey Gingerbread

(100 yr old recipe)

Ingredients

- 3 c self-rising flour *(you'll be adding more)*
- 3 heaping Tbsp ground ginger
- 2 heaping tsp cinnamon
- 2 tsp baking soda
- 1 c vegetable oil
- 1 c buttermilk
- 1 c molasses
- 3 c sugar
- 4 eggs, plus 1 extra yolk *(save the white to brush the top)*

Directions

1. Preheat oven to 375°F. Grease cookie sheets and set aside.
2. In a large bowl, combine the self-rising flour, ginger, cinnamon, and baking soda. Set aside.
3. In another bowl, combine the vegetable oil, buttermilk, molasses, sugar, eggs, and egg yolk. Mix well till smooth.
4. Make a well in the center of the dry ingredients and pour in the wet mixture. Stir till fully combined.
5. Gradually add more flour, one cup at a time, till a stiff dough forms. When it becomes difficult to stir with a spoon, it's ready.
6. Turn the dough out onto a floured surface and knead gently till smooth.
7. Form 1½-inch balls and place about six per greased baking sheet. Flatten each ball with your palm to about ½-inch thick large cookies.
8. Brush the tops with the reserved egg white for a glossy finish.

9. Bake for 8–10 minutes for softer cookies or a few minutes longer for more cake-like cookies.
10. Cool on a wire rack to allow cookies to set. Store in an airtight container at room temperature.

Variation: *For a bread-style gingerbread, do not add the extra flour. Pour the batter into a greased 9x13-inch pan and bake at 350°F for 20–25 minutes, or in two loaf pans for 30–35 minutes at the same temperature, till a toothpick inserted in the center comes out clean.*

Hummingbird Cake

Ingredients

- 3 c all-purpose flour, plus more for dusting pans
- 2 c sugar
- 1 tsp each: salt, cinnamon & baking soda
- 3 large eggs, room temperature and slightly beaten
- 1½ c vegetable oil
- 1½ tsp vanilla extract
- 1 *(8 oz)* can crushed pineapple, undrained
- 2 c chopped ripe bananas *(about 4 medium)*
- 1 c toasted pecans, chopped
- 1 recipe Cream Cheese Frosting

Directions

1. Preheat the oven to 350°F.
2. Grease and lightly flour three 9-inch round cake pans; set aside.

Prepare the Batter/Cake Layers

3. In a large mixing bowl, whisk together the flour, sugar, salt, baking soda, and cinnamon.
4. Add the eggs and oil, stirring just till the dry ingredients are moistened.
5. Stir in the vanilla extract, crushed pineapple (with juice), chopped bananas, and toasted pecans till evenly combined.

Bake the Layers

6. Divide batter evenly among 3 prepared 9-inch round pans.
7. Bake for 25–30 minutes, or till a wooden pick inserted into the center comes out clean.
8. Cool the cakes in the pans on wire racks for 10 minutes. Then remove from the pans and allow to cool completely on the racks.

Frost the Cake

9. Prepare the Cream Cheese Frosting (see recipe).
10. Place the first cake layer on a serving platter and spread with 1 cup of frosting.
11. Repeat with the remaining layers, then frost the top and sides of the cake.

Garnish

12. Arrange pecan halves decoratively on top of the cake in a circular pattern.

Chocolate Éclair Cake

Ingredients

- 1 *(14.4-ounce)* box graham crackers
- 2 *(3.4-ounce)* packages instant French vanilla pudding mix
- 2½ c whole milk
- 1 *(12-ounce)* container whipped topping *(such as Cool Whip)*, thawed

Frosting

- ⅓ c chocolate chips
- 2 tsps corn syrup
- 1 tsp vanilla extract
- 3 Tbsp unsalted butter, softened
- 1½ c powdered sugar
- 3 Tbsp whole milk

Directions

Prepare the Pudding Layer

1. In a medium mixing bowl, whisk together the pudding mix and milk till slightly thickened.
2. Gently fold in the thawed whipped topping till smooth and combined.

Create the Cake

3. In a 13x9-inch dish, arrange a single layer of graham crackers on the bottom.
4. Spread half of the pudding mixture evenly over the crackers.
5. Repeat the layers--graham crackers followed by pudding--till the dish is full, ending with a final layer of graham crackers on top.

Make the Frosting

6. In a small saucepan over medium-low heat, combine the chocolate chips and corn syrup. Stir till melted and smooth.
7. Remove from heat and whisk in the vanilla, butter, milk, and powdered sugar till creamy and well blended.

Finish & Chill

8. Spread the frosting evenly over the top graham cracker layer.
9. Cover and refrigerate overnight to allow the crackers to soften before serving.

Tip: *For a quicker option, substitute canned chocolate frosting. Warm it in the microwave for about 30 seconds, stir till smooth, and spread over the top of the cake before chilling.*

Missy's Prize-Winning Chocolate Cake

Ingredients

- 3 c all-purpose flour
- 2½ c sugar
- 1½ c unsweetened baking cocoa
- 1 Tbsp baking soda
- 1½ tsp baking powder
- 1½ tsp salt
- 4 large eggs, room temperature
- 1½ c buttermilk, room temperature
- 1½ c warm strong brewed coffee or warm water
- ½ c vegetable oil
- 2 tsp vanilla extract
- 1 recipe Vanilla Buttercream
- *(see page)*
- 1 recipe Chocolate Ganache
- *(see page)*

Directions

1. Preheat the oven to 350°F.
2. Grease and flour three 9-inch round cake pans.

Prepare the batter

3. In the bowl of a stand mixer, combine the flour, sugar, cocoa, baking powder, and salt. Mix on low speed till blended.

Add Wet Ingredients

4. Add the eggs, buttermilk, water (or coffee), oil, and vanilla extract. Beat on medium speed till the batter is smooth—this should take about 2 minutes. *Do not overmix.*

Bake the cakes

5. Divide the batter evenly among the prepared pans. Bake for 30–35 minutes, or till a toothpick inserted in the center comes out clean.

Cool

6. Allow the cakes to cool in the pans on wire racks for 15 minutes. Then, carefully remove from the pans and cool completely on the racks.

Assemble

7. Once cooled, frost between the layers and over the top and sides with vanilla buttercream.

Finish

8. Chill the frosted cake for about 1 hour, then pour the chocolate ganache over the top, allowing it to gently drizzle down the sides.

Chocolate Ganache

Ingredients

- 1 c semi-sweet chocolate chips
- 1 c heavy whipping cream
- 1 Tbsp light corn syrup

Directions

1. In a saucepan, heat the heavy cream over medium heat till it's just about to boil.
2. Remove from heat and pour the hot cream over the chocolate chips and corn syrup in a heatproof bowl.
3. Let stand for 2 minutes, then whisk till smooth and fully melted.
4. Allow the ganache to cool for about 15 minutes, then pour over a chilled cake.
5. Let cool for 15 minutes and pour over chilled cake.

Tip: *This recipe also makes a great whipped frosting. Let cool completely to room temperature and beat on high speed with a mixer till fluffy.*

Perfect for any cake — I use this on my German Chocolate Cake.

Recipe can be doubled.

Molasses Cake

Ingredients

- ½ c shortening
- 1 c boiling water
- ½ c sugar
- 1 c molasses
- 2 tsp baking soda
- ¼ tsp salt
- 1 tsp cinnamon
- 1 tsp ground ginger
- 1 tsp ground cloves
- 2½ c all-purpose flour, sifted
- 1 egg, well beaten

Directions

1. Preheat oven to 350°F.
2. Spray a 9x13-inch baking dish with nonstick cooking spray and set aside.
3. In a large mixing bowl, combine the shortening and boiling water. Stir till the shortening melts.
4. Add the sugar and molasses, mixing till well combined.
5. In a separate bowl, sift together the flour, baking soda, salt, cinnamon, ginger, and cloves.
6. Gradually add the dry ingredients to the wet mixture, stirring till incorporated. Add the beaten egg and mix till the batter is smooth and well combined.
7. Pour the batter into the prepared baking dish and bake for 30–40 minutes, or till a toothpick inserted in the center comes out clean. *Be careful not to overbake.*
8. Let the cake cool before serving. Enjoy plain, topped with whipped cream, or frosted with cream cheese frosting.

Orange Slice Cake

Ingredients

- 1 c butter, softened
- 2 c white sugar
- 4 eggs
- ½ c buttermilk
- 1 tsp baking soda
- 3 ½ c all-purpose flour
- 1 pound pitted dates, chopped
- 1 pound orange slice candy, chopped
- 2 c chopped pecans
- 1⅓ c shredded coconut
- 1 c orange juice
- 2 c confectioners' sugar

Directions

1. Preheat oven to 250°F. Lightly grease and flour a 10-inch tube pan.

Cream the Butter and Sugar

2. In a large mixing bowl, cream together the butter and sugar till light and smooth.
3. Add the eggs one at a time, beating well after each addition.

Mix Wet Ingredients

4. Dissolve the baking soda in the buttermilk, then add to the creamed mixture, stirring till fully combined.

Prepare Dry Mixture

5. In a separate large bowl, combine the flour, chopped dates, orange slice candy, and pecans. Stir well to coat each piece with flour.

Combine Mixtures

6. Add the flour mixture and shredded coconut to the creamed mixture. *This makes very stiff dough, so it is necessary to stir with a wooden spoon till the stiff batter forms.*

Bake

7. Pour the batter into the prepared pan and bake for 2½ to 3 hours, or till a toothpick inserted in the center comes out clean.

Glaze

8. Immediately after removing the cake from the oven, combine the orange juice and confectioners' sugar. Pour over the hot cake.

Cool

9. Allow the cake to stand in the pan overnight before serving.

German Chocolate Cake with Coconut Pecan Frosting

Ingredients

Cake

- 1 box German chocolate cake mix

Frosting

- 1⅓ c evaporated milk
- 1⅓ c sugar
- 1 stick *(½cup)* unsalted butter, room temperature
- 2 eggs, slightly beaten
- 1 c toasted pecans
- 2 c sweetened flaked coconut
- 1 tsp vanilla extract
- Optional Topping: Whipped chocolate ganache

Note: *I make many cakes from scratch, but when it comes to German Chocolate Cake, I've found that a good box cake mix works just as well--but I always use homemade frosting.*

Prepare the Cake

1. Preheat oven to 350°F (or as directed on the cake mix box).

2. Prepare the cake batter according to the package instructions, substituting buttermilk for the water to give it a richer flavor and softer crumb.
3. Divide the batter evenly between two greased 8-inch round pans sprayed with nonstick cooking spray.
4. Bake according to the package directions, or till a toothpick inserted in the center comes out clean.
5. Cool the cakes in the pans for 10 minutes, then transfer to a wire rack to cool completely.

Make the Frosting

6. In a medium saucepan over medium-high heat, combine the evaporated milk, sugar, butter, and eggs. Cook and stir continuously for 6–8 minutes, or till the mixture thickens.
7. Remove from heat and stir in the pecans, coconut, and vanilla. Allow the frosting to cool till slightly warm—it will be easier to spread.

Tip: *If the frosting becomes too thick or dry (which can happen if it's overboiled), drizzle in a little extra milk and stir till it reaches a smooth, spreadable consistency.*

Assemble the Cake

8. Frost the layers, outside and top of the cake.

Optional

9. Pipe whipped chocolate ganache or frosting around the bottom and top edges of the cake.

This is my hubby's favorite cake.

Doctored-Up Cake Mix

Ingredients

- 1 box cake mix *(any flavor)*
- ¾ c buttermilk, room-temperature
- 1 tsp vanilla extract
- ⅓ c sour cream
- ½ c vegetable oil
- 4 eggs, room-temperature

Directions

1. Preheat oven according to the temperature listed on the cake mix box.
2. In a large mixing bowl, combine all ingredients and mix till just combined. *Do not overmix.*
3. Pour the batter into prepared pans and bake according to the directions on the box.
4. Cool completely before frosting or serving.

Doctored-Up Chocolate Cake Mix

Ingredients

- 1 box chocolate cake mix *(any brand)*
- 4 eggs, room-temperature
- ½ c vegetable oil
- 1½ cu brewed coffee or buttermilk, room temperature
- ⅓ c sour cream
- 3 Tbsp dark unsweetened baking cocoa
- 1 tsp vanilla or coffee extract

Directions

1. Preheat the oven according to the temperature listed on the cake mix box.
2. In a large mixing bowl, combine all ingredients and mix till just combined. *Do not overmix.*
3. Pour the batter into prepared pans and bake according to the directions on the box.
4. Allow the cake to cool completely before frosting or serving.

***Note:** The coffee enhances the chocolate flavor without adding a coffee taste. If preferred, you can substitute buttermilk and vanilla extract for the coffee and coffee extract.*

White Wedding Cake

Ingredients

- 1 *(15.25 oz)* box white cake mix
- 1 c all-purpose flour
- ¾ tsp salt
- 1⅓ c water
- 1 c granulated sugar
- 1 c sour cream
- ½ tsp pure vanilla extract
- 1 tsp pure almond extract
- 2 Tbsp avocado oil *(or vegetable oil)*
- 4 large egg whites, room temperature

Directions

1. Preheat oven to 325°F.
2. In a large mixing bowl, combine all ingredients and mix till smooth and just combined. *Do not overmix.*
3. Spray two 9-inch round or three 8-inch round cake pans with nonstick baking spray (I use Baker's Joy). Divide the batter evenly among the pans.
4. Bake for 30–40 minutes, or till a toothpick inserted into the center comes out clean. *Avoid overbaking.*
5. Allow the cakes to cool in the pans for 10 minutes, then turn out onto wire racks to cool completely.
6. Frost with **Vanilla Swiss Meringue Buttercream**, **Boiled Vanilla Frosting**, or **Classic Vanilla Buttercream**, as desired.

Old Fashioned Chocolate Pie

Ingredients

Pie Crust

- 1 *(9-inch)* baked pie crust

Filling

- 2 c evaporated milk
- 1 c sugar
- ¼ c corn starch
- 3 egg yolks
- ½ c cocoa powder
- ¼ tsp salt
- 1 tsp pure vanilla extract
- 1 tbs unsalted butter, softened

Directions

1. In a medium saucepan over medium heat, combine all the filling ingredients except the vanilla and butter.
2. Whisk together and continue whisking constantly till the mixture comes to a boil and begins to thicken.
3. Once thickened, remove from heat and stir in the butter and vanilla till fully combined.
4. Pour the filling into the pre-baked pie crust, spreading evenly.
5. Cool at room temperature, then refrigerate for several hours.
6. Top with whipped cream and chocolate shavings, or finish with a meringue topping if desired.

Matilda Cake with Chocolate Fudge Frosting

Ingredients

- 1 box chocolate cake mix (*any brand*)
- 4 eggs, room-temperature
- ½ c vegetable oil
- 1½ cu brewed coffee or buttermilk, room temperature
- ⅓ c sour cream
- 3 Tbsp dark unsweetened baking cocoa
- 1 tsp vanilla or coffee extract

Directions

1. Preheat the oven according to the temperature listed on the cake mix box.
2. In a large mixing bowl, combine all ingredients and mix till just combined. *Do not overmix.*
3. Pour the batter into prepared pans and bake according to the directions on the box.
4. Allow the cake to cool completely before frosting or serving.

Note: *The coffee enhances the chocolate flavor without adding a coffee taste. If preferred, you can substitute buttermilk and vanilla extract for the coffee and coffee extract.*

Chocolate Fudge Frosting

Ingredients

- 1 *(8 oz)* block cream cheese, softened
- 1 stick unsalted butter, softened
- 1 c dark chocolate chips
- 1 tsp vanilla or coffee extract
- ½ c dark baking cocoa
- 2½–3 c powdered sugar
- ½ c whole milk, heavy cream, or half-and-half *(enough to reach desired spreading consistency)*

Directions

1. In a large bowl using a hand or stand mixer, beat the cream cheese and butter together till light and fluffy.
2. In a microwave-safe bowl, melt the chocolate chips in 20–30 second intervals, stirring between each, till smooth and melted.
3. Add the melted chocolate to the cream cheese mixture and mix till well combined.
4. Mix in the vanilla or coffee extract.
5. Gradually add the powdered sugar, a little at a time, while drizzling in the milk till you get a smooth, spreadable consistency.
6. Frost the top and sides of the cake.
7. Cover and chill before serving, or serve at room temperature.

Lane Cake

Ingredients

For the Cake

- 6 large egg whites
- ¾ c butter, softened
- 1½ c sugar
- 1 tsp vanilla extract
- 2¼ c all-purpose flour
- 2½ tsp baking powder
- ½ tsp salt
- ¾ c 2% milk

For the Filling

- 6 large egg yolks
- 1 c sugar
- ½ c butter, cubed
- ¼ c bourbon
- 1 Tbsp grated orange zest
- ¼ tsp salt
- ¾ c raisins
- ¾ c sweetened shredded coconut
- ¾ c chopped pecans
- ¾ c coarsely chopped red candied cherries
- 1 c heavy whipping cream, whipped and sweetened

Directions

1. Grease three 9-inch round baking pans, line the bottoms with parchment paper, and grease the parchment. Set aside.
2. Place the egg whites in a large bowl and let stand at room temperature for 30 minutes.
3. In another large bowl, cream together the butter and sugar till light and fluffy. Beat in the vanilla extract.

4. In a separate bowl, whisk together the flour, baking powder, and salt. Add the dry mixture to the creamed mixture alternately with the milk, beating well after each addition.
5. Beat the egg whites till stiff peaks form, then gently fold them into the batter. Divide the batter evenly among the prepared pans.
6. Bake at 325°F for 20-25 minutes, or till a toothpick inserted in the center comes out clean.
7. Cool in pans for 10 minutes before transferring to wire racks. Remove parchment paper and let cool completely.

Prepare the Filling

8. In a large saucepan, whisk together the egg yolks and sugar.
9. Add the butter and cook over medium-low heat, stirring constantly, till the sugar dissolves and the mixture thickens *(do not boil)*.
10. Remove from heat and stir in the bourbon, orange zest, and salt. Fold in the raisins, coconut, pecans, and candied cherries. Let cool completely.

Assemble the Cake

11. Place one cake layer on a serving plate and spread with one-third of the filling.
12. Repeat with remaining layers and filling.
13. Frost the sides of the cake with sweetened whipped cream.
14. Refrigerate till ready to serve.

Swiss Meringue Buttercream

Ingredients

- 5 egg whites, at room temperature
- 2 c unsalted butter, at room temperature
- 1½ c extra fine granulated sugar
- Pinch of salt
- 1 tsp pure vanilla extract
- ½ tsp almond extract *(Optional)*

Directions

1. In a clean mixing bowl, combine the egg whites, sugar, and salt, and whisk briefly to blend. (I used the bowl from my stand mixer.)
2. Set the bowl over a pot of gently simmering water, making sure the bottom of the bowl does not touch the water.
3. Whisk occasionally while the mixture warms, then whisk constantly once it begins to heat.
4. Continue till the mixture reaches 160°F or till the sugar has dissolved and no longer feels grainy when rubbed between your fingers.
5. Transfer the bowl to a stand mixer fitted with the whisk attachment.
6. Beat on high speed till the meringue forms stiff, glossy peaks and the bowl has cooled to room temperature.

7. Switch to the paddle attachment. With the mixer on low speed, add the butter one tablespoon dollop, a little at a time, allowing each addition to fully incorporate before adding more.
8. Once all the butter has been added, pour in the vanilla (and almond extract, if using). Increase the speed to medium-high and beat till the frosting is smooth.
9. If the frosting appears curdled or loose after adding the butter, continue beating till it comes together and becomes smooth.

The recipe makes enough to frost two 8- or 9-inch round layer cakes or one 9x13-inch cake.

Store covered in the refrigerator for up to one week or freeze for up to six months.

Kentucky Dried Apple Stack Cake

Ingredients

Apple Filling

- 2 lbs dried apples
- 1-2 heaping tsp cinnamon or apple pie spice *(to taste)*
- 1 c sugar or sweetener of choice *(add an additional ½ cup dark brown sugar for a sweeter, darker filling)*
- 4-6 cups water *(add more as needed while cooking)*

Cake Layers:

- ½ c veg shortening
- ½ c sugar
- 1 egg
- ⅓ c sorghum
- ½ c buttermilk
- 1 tsp vanilla extract
- 3½ c all-purpose flour
- ½ tsp baking soda
- ½ tsp salt
- 1 tsp ground ginger

Directions

For the Filling

1. Place the dried apples in a heavy kettle and add 4 cups of water to start.
2. Bring to a simmer over medium heat.
3. Reduce heat to medium-low, cover, and cook for about 10 minutes.

4. Uncover and stir. Add more water if needed—some apples absorb more water than others.
5. Cover and cook for another 10 minutes, then repeat this process till the apples are tender and beginning to fall apart.
6. Mash the apples till thick but not dry. I mash mine with a potato masher.
7. Stir in the sugar and spices, then remove from heat.
8. Add the sugar and spices. stir and remove from heat.
9. Set aside to cool slightly while you prepare the cake layers.

Layers

10. Preheat the oven to 350°F.
11. In a small bowl, combine the flour, baking soda, ginger, and salt. Mix well and set aside.
12. In a mixing bowl, cream together the shortening and sugar for about 2–5 minutes.
13. Add the egg, sorghum, and vanilla extract, and mix till well combined.
14. Reduce the mixer speed to low and gradually add the flour mixture, a little at a time, as you drizzle in the buttermilk. Continue mixing till the dough comes together.
15. Turn the dough out onto a floured surface and shape it into a log about 10 inches long.
16. Cut the log into 7 equal pieces and roll each into a round ball.
17. Spray a 9-inch round pan with baking spray (with flour) and press one dough ball evenly into the bottom of the pan.
18. Bake each layer for 10–15 minutes, or till lightly browned. (Using multiple pans, I like to bake 4 pans at a time.)
19. Allow each layer to cool in the pan briefly, then turn out onto a wire rack to cool completely.

20. Once cooled, begin assembling the cake. Spread about 1 cup of warm apple filling between each layer, repeating till all layers are used. (I like to use warm filling because it ensures the cake will not be dry.)
21. Top the cake with additional apples if desired, or leave plain and dust with powdered sugar before serving.
22. Cover the cake and let it rest for 24 hours to allow the flavors to meld, the layers to soften and for it to absorb all the goodness.

Optional: *Refrigeration is optional. My Great Aunt Lucy kept hers on the table for 3-4 days till it was gone. Enjoy!*

Tip: *Substitute apple butter or apple sauce for dried apples.*

Old Timey 7 Minute Frosting

Ingredients

- 5 egg whites, room temperature
- 1 c sugar
- 1/8 tsp cream of tarter
- 1 tsp pure vanilla extract

Directions

1. In a large metal mixing bowl, combine all ingredients and stir to blend.
2. Place the bowl over a saucepan of simmering water on low heat, creating a double boiler.
3. Heat and stir constantly till the sugar is completely dissolved. To test, rub a small amount between your fingers—there should be no graininess.
4. Remove the bowl from the heat and, using a stand mixer fitted with a whisk attachment, begin whipping the egg whites on low speed.
5. Gradually increase the speed to high and continue whipping for about 7 minutes, or till the mixture is glossy, thick, and forms stiff peaks.

Tip: *This frosting is great on coconut, white, yellow, chocolate, or angel food cake.*

Browned Butter Frosting

Ingredients

- 1½ c salted butter, at room temperature, cut into pieces
- 1½ lbs powdered sugar
- ½ Tbsp pure vanilla extract or maple extract
- 1-2 Tbsp heavy cream or whole milk

Directions

1. In a light-colored heavy Dutch oven or skillet over medium heat, add the butter. Melt completely, stirring often.
2. As the butter cooks, it will foam and then subside. You'll hear sputtering as the water evaporates.
3. When the foaming decreases, watch for brown specks forming on the bottom of the pan and a nutty aroma developing.
4. As the butter begins to brown, watch it closely, because it will burn quickly.
5. Once the butter reaches a golden brown color, remove it from the heat immediately to prevent burning.
6. Let the browned butter cool completely to room temperature.
7. Once cooled, transfer the butter to a mixing bowl.
8. Add the powdered sugar and beat with the whisk attachment on medium speed for 3–4 minutes, scraping down the sides as needed.
9. Add the vanilla extract and cream. Mix on low speed for 1–2 minutes, then increase to medium-high and beat for about 5 minutes till light and fluffy.

10. If the frosting is too thick, drizzle in milk a little at a time till it reaches the desired consistency.
11. For an ultra-smooth texture, switch to the paddle attachment and beat briefly.

This frosting pairs beautifully with spice cake, apple cake, or even chocolate chip cookies.

3. Slowly drizzle about ¼ cup of the hot milk mixture into the egg yolk mixture, whisking vigorously to prevent curdling.
4. Gradually drizzle the tempered egg mixture back into the saucepan, whisking continuously.

Cook the Custard

5. Continue cooking over medium-low heat, stirring constantly, till the custard thickens.
6. Remove from heat and stir in the butter, vanilla extract, and coconut extract till smooth.
7. Fold in the shredded coconut.

Assemble the Pie

8. Pour the warm custard into the pre-baked pie shell.
9. Let cool completely at room temperature, then cover with plastic wrap and refrigerate for at least 4 hours or overnight.

Make the Whipped Topping

10. In a clean, chilled mixing bowl, combine the cold heavy cream, powdered sugar, and coconut extract.
11. Whisk on high till stiff peaks form.

Finish and Serve

12. Spread the whipped cream evenly over the chilled pie.
13. Sprinkle toasted coconut over the top for garnish.

Kentucky Butter Cake

Ingredients

Cake

- 3 c all-purpose four
- 2 c sugar
- 1 tsp salt
- 1 tsp baking powder
- ½ tsp baking soda
- 1 c buttermilk
- 4 eggs, room temperature
- 1 Tbsp vanilla
- 1 c unsalted butter, softened

Glaze

- ¾ c sugar
- ⅓ c butter
- 1 Tbsp vanilla
- 2 Tbsp water

Directions

1. Preheat oven to 325°F.
2. In a medium bowl, whisk together the flour, salt, baking powder, and baking soda. Set aside.
3. In a large mixing bowl, beat the sugar, butter, and vanilla together till light and well combined.
4. Add the eggs, then mix in the buttermilk till smooth.
5. Add the dry ingredients, a little at a time, to the wet mixture, beating for 2–3 minutes till the batter is smooth and creamy.
6. Pour the batter into a well-greased Bundt pan and smooth the top evenly.
7. Bake for 60–70 minutes, or till a toothpick inserted into the center comes out clean.

8. Once baked, poke holes across the top of the cake and allow it to cool in the pan.
9. To make the glaze, melt the butter in a saucepan over medium-low heat. Add the sugar, water, and vanilla, stirring constantly till the sugar dissolves. *Do not boil.*
10. Pour the warm glaze over the cake while it's still in the pan, allowing it to soak in for at least 20 minutes.
11. Carefully flip the cake onto a serving plate, slice, and serve.

Coconut Custard Pie

Ingredients

- 1 *(9-inch)* pre-baked pie crust

For the Filling

- 3 c half & half
- ¾ c sugar
- 4 egg yolks
- 3 heaping Tbsp cornstarch
- 1 tsp coconut extract
- 1 tsp vanilla extract
- 1 Tbsp salted butter
- 1½ cups sweetened shredded coconut

For the Topping

- 2 c cold heavy whipping cream
- 2 Tbsp powdered sugar
- ½ tsp coconut extract
- ½ c toasted coconut

Directions

Prepare the Filling

1. In a small bowl, whisk together the egg yolks and cornstarch. Set aside.
2. In a heavy saucepan over medium heat, combine the half & half and sugar. Stir frequently and bring just to a simmer.

Temper the Eggs

Butterscotch Cream Pie

Ingredients

For the Pie

- 1 *(9-inch)* pre-baked pie crust *(graham cracker or traditional)*
- 1½ c packed brown sugar
- ⅓ c self-rising flour
- 2¼ c whole milk
- 3 egg yolks, slightly beaten
- 2 Tbsp unsalted butter, softened
- 1 tsp vanilla extract
- ½ tsp maple extract *(my secret ingredient, but optional)*

For the Whipped Topping

- 2 c heavy whipping cream
- 2 Tbsp powdered sugar
- ¼ tsp vanilla extract ***or*** one *(8 oz)* container whipped topping

Directions

Cook the Filling

1. In a heavy saucepan over medium heat, whisk together the brown sugar, flour, milk, and egg yolks till smooth.
2. Bring the mixture to a gentle boil, then reduce the heat to low. Continue cooking for about 4 minutes, stirring constantly, till the custard thickens and becomes smooth.

Add Flavorings

3. Remove from heat and stir in the softened butter, vanilla extract, and maple extract (if using) till fully combined and silky.

Assemble the Pie

4. Pour the warm custard into the pre-baked pie shell.
5. Let the pie cool at room temperature for 1 hour, then refrigerate for 2–3 hours.

Prepare the Whipped Topping

6. In a mixing bowl, combine the heavy cream, powdered sugar, and vanilla extract.
7. Beat on high speed till stiff peaks form.
   (Alternatively, use an 8-ounce container of whipped topping.)

Finish and Serve

8. Spread the whipped topping evenly over the chilled pie.
9. Options: Sprinkle with toffee pieces, butterscotch chips or pecan pieces.

Coco-Cola Cake

Ingredients

Cake

- 1 box chocolate cake mix
- 2 large eggs
- 12 oz cola

Frosting

- ½ cup unsalted butter
- 3 Tbsp cocoa powder
- 6 Tbsp cola soda
- 4 c powdered sugar
- 1 tsp vanilla extract

Directions

1. Preheat oven to 350°F.
2. In a large bowl, add the cake mix, eggs, and cola. Stir till well combined.
3. Pour the mixture into a greased 9x13-inch pan.
4. Bake for 30–35 minutes, or till a toothpick inserted in the center comes out clean.

To Make the Frosting

5. Combine the butter, cocoa powder, and cola in a saucepan.
6. Heat over medium heat till the mixture begins to boil slightly, then remove from the heat.
7. Whisk in the powdered sugar and vanilla till smooth.
8. Pour the frosting over the warm cake and let it set before serving.

Fried Apple Pies (Hand Pies)

Ingredients

Dough

- 2 c self-rising flour
- ¼ c lard
- ¾ c buttermilk *(or enough to make a thick dough)*

Apple Filling

- 6 apples, peeled and sliced *(I use Granny Smith.)*
- 1 c sugar
- ½ stick unsalted butter, room temperature
- ¼ c water
- Dash of cinnamon
- 1 ½ Tbsp water
- 1 tsp corn starch

For Frying

- Vegetable oil

Directions

Make Filling

1. Place apples, sugar, butter, water, and cinnamon in a saucepan.
2. Cook and stir over medium heat till the apples are tender, about 10–15 minutes.
3. To thicken, mix the water and cornstarch together in a small cup, then pour into the simmering apples. Stir till slightly thickened, then remove from heat and let cool completely.
4. For the dough, cut the lard into the flour till crumbly.
5. Add buttermilk and mix till a thick dough forms.

6. Turn the dough out onto a floured surface and knead in additional flour till stiff and smooth.
7. Roll the dough out thinly and cut into 6-inch round pieces.
8. Place about 2 spoonfuls of the apple filling in the center of each round piece (don't overfill).
9. Fold each round into a half-moon shape and seal the edges with a fork.
10. Heat about 1 inch of oil in a skillet over medium heat.
11. Fry pies for 2–3 minutes on each side, till golden brown. *I use two spatulas to flip the pies.*
12. Drain on paper towels or wire racks.
13. Dust with powdered sugar before serving.

Optional: *Substitute with any fruit or pudding filling of your choice.*

Peanut Butter Pretzel Pie

Ingredients

For the Crust

- 2½ cups pretzels
- ½ cup sugar
- 10 Tbsp unsalted butter, melted

For the Filling:

- 8 oz cream cheese, softened
- ½ can sweetened condensed milk *(Tip: save the remaining half for coffee creamer.)*
- 1 *(8 oz)* tub whipped topping
- 1 c creamy peanut butter
- 1 small jar hot fudge sauce, slightly warmed
- 1 c finely chopped chocolate-covered pretzels

Directions

Prepare the Crust

1. Place the pretzels in a zip-top bag or food processor. Crush or pulse with a rolling pin till coarse crumbs form.
2. In a bowl, combine the pretzel crumbs and sugar. Pour in the melted butter and stir till evenly coated.
3. Press the mixture firmly into a 9-inch deep-dish pie pan, making sure to press up along the sides.
4. Chill for about 1 hour.

Make the Filling

5. In a large mixing bowl, beat the cream cheese and sweetened condensed milk together till smooth.
6. Gently fold in the whipped topping till fully combined. Set aside.

Combine the Peanut Butter Swirl

7. In a separate bowl, mix together the peanut butter and warm fudge sauce till smooth.

Assemble the Pie

8. Pour half of the cream cheese mixture into the chilled pretzel crust.
9. Drop half of the peanut butter mixture over top by the spoonful and swirl gently.
10. Sprinkle with some of the chopped chocolate-covered pretzels.
11. Repeat with the remaining cream cheese and peanut butter mixtures, then top with the remaining chopped pretzels.

Chill and Serve

12. Freeze the pie for at least 6 hours or overnight till firm.
13. Keep refrigerated or frozen till ready to serve.

Lemon Meringue Pie

Ingredients

- 1 *(9-inch)* pre-baked pie crust
- 5 large egg yolks *(reserve the whites for the meringue)*
- 1 and ⅓ c water
- 1 c granulated sugar
- ⅓ c cornstarch
- ¼ tsp salt
- ½ c fresh lemon juice
- 1 Tbsp lemon zest
- 2 Tbsp unsalted butter

Meringue

- 5 large egg whites, at room temperature
- ½ tsp cream of tartar
- ½ c granulated sugar
- 1/8 tsp salt

Directions

Make the Filling

1. Whisk the egg yolks together in a medium bowl or liquid measuring cup. Set aside.
2. In a medium saucepan over medium heat, whisk together the water, sugar, cornstarch, salt, lemon juice, and lemon zest. Cook till the mixture thickens and begins to bubble, about 6 minutes. Once thickened, whisk again and reduce the heat to low.
3. Temper the egg yolks by slowly streaming a few spoonfuls of the warm lemon mixture into the beaten yolks, whisking constantly. Then, in a slow stream, whisk the egg yolk mixture back into the saucepan.

4. Increase the heat to medium and cook till the filling is thick and large bubbles burst at the surface.
5. Remove from heat and whisk in the butter.
6. Spread the hot filling into the warm partially baked pie crust.
7. Do not let the filling cool completely before adding the meringue—keeping it warm helps to seal the layers and prevent separation.
8. Set aside as you prepare the meringue.

Make the Meringue

9. Using a handheld mixer or stand mixer fitted with a whisk attachment, beat the egg whites and cream of tartar together on medium speed for 1 minute. Increase to high speed and beat till soft peaks form, about 4 minutes.
10. Add sugar and salt, then continue beating on high speed till glossy stiff peaks form, about 2 more minutes.
11. Spread the meringue over the warm filling. (I like to make decorative peaks with the back of a large spoon.) Be sure to spread it all the way to the crust's edge to prevent weeping.

Bake the Pie

12. Bake the pie on the lowest oven rack for 20–25 minutes, till the meringue is golden brown. If it begins to brown too quickly, tent loosely with foil without touching the meringue.
13. Remove from the oven and cool on a wire rack for 1 hour.
14. Refrigerate for at least 4 hours before slicing and serving.

Kenzie's Dutch Apple Pie

Ingredients

Pie Crust

- 1 *(9-inch)* deep-dish unbaked frozen pie crust, thawed

Filling

- 7 Granny Smith apples, peeled and thinly sliced
- 1 Tbsp fresh lemon juice
- ¼ c granulated sugar
- ¼ c packed brown sugar
- 3 Tbsp all-purpose flour
- 1 Tbsp apple pie spice
- Pinch of salt

Crumb Topping

- 1 c all-purpose flour
- ½ c granulated sugar
- ½ c packed brown sugar
- 1 tsp ground cinnamon
- ½ c salted butter, softened

Directions

Crumb Topping

1. In a bowl, mix all the crumb topping ingredients together with a fork till crumbly. Set aside.

For the Filling

2. Preheat oven to 425°F.
3. In a large bowl, combine all the filling ingredients, tossing till the apples are well coated.

4. Pour the filling into the thawed pie crust, then evenly sprinkle the crumb topping over the apples.
5. Bake uncovered for 10 minutes.
6. Reduce the oven temperature to 350°F, cover the pie loosely with foil to prevent the sugar from burning, and bake for 30–40 minutes.
7. Uncover and bake an additional 10–15 minutes, or till the topping is golden brown.
8. Let the pie cool for about 30 minutes before slicing.
9. Serve warm with ice cream or whipped cream.

Cherry Cheesecake Pie (No-Bake)

Ingredients

- 1 *(8 oz)* package cream cheese, softened
- 1 *(14 oz)* can sweetened condensed milk
- ⅓ c lemon juice
- 1 tsp vanilla extract
- 1 *(9-inch)* graham cracker crust
- 1 can chilled cherry pie filling *(or any fruit filling of your choice)*

Directions

1. In a large bowl, combine the cream cheese, condensed milk, lemon juice, and vanilla. Mix till creamy and smooth.
2. Pour the mixture into the graham cracker crust and spread evenly.
3. Cover with plastic wrap and refrigerate for several hours.
4. Pour the fruit pie filling over the chilled pie.
5. Refrigerate for an additional 1–2 hours before serving.

DESSERTS

Mommy's Blackberry Dumplins

Ingredients

Filling

- 2 lbs frozen blackberries (*or any berries or peaches*)
- 2 c sugar
- ½ stick unsalted butter, room temperature
- Enough water to cover the berries (*about 2 inches above*)

Dumplings

- 2 c self-rising flour
- ⅓ c unsalted butter, melted
- Enough whole milk to make a dough

Directions

Prepare the Filling

1. In a large heavy saucepan over medium heat, combine the berries, water, sugar, and butter.
2. Cook and stir gently until the mixture comes to a boil.

Prepare the Dumplings

3. To make the dumplings, place the flour in a mixing bowl and make a well in the center.
4. Pour in the melted butter and gradually drizzle in milk, stirring just until a sticky dough forms.

5. Lightly sprinkle flour over the dough and your hands. Pinch off small portions and roll into 2-inch balls.

Cook the Dumplings in the Filling

6. Drop the dumplings gently into the boiling berries without stirring.
7. Use a spoon to move the dumplings slightly to make room for each one.
8. Reduce the heat to low, cover, and simmer for about 10 minutes.
9. Serve warm with ice cream or whipped cream.

Strawberry Cream Cheese Cobbler

Ingredients

- 2 cans crescent dinner rolls
- 1 can strawberry pie filling *(or any pie filling)*
- 1 *(8 oz)* block cream cheese, softened
- 2 Tbsp butter, melted
- 3 tsp sugar

Directions

1. Preheat oven to 350°F.
2. Butter a 9x9-inch baking dish.
3. Unfold one can of crescent rolls and press into the bottom of the pan, sealing the seams.
4. Evenly spread the softened cream cheese over the dough, all the way to the edges.
5. Pour the strawberry pie filling over the cream cheese layer and spread evenly.
6. Unfold the second can of crescent rolls and spread it gently over the strawberry filling.
7. Brush the top with melted butter and sprinkle evenly with sugar.
8. Bake for 30–40 minutes, or until golden brown and bubbly.
9. Cool slightly before slicing and serve warm or at room temperature.

Mommy's Banana Pudding

Ingredients

- 1 *(14 oz)* can sweetened condensed milk
- 2 c cold whole milk
- 1 *(3.4 oz)* box French vanilla instant pudding
- 2 *(8 oz)* containers whipped topping *(I use "extra creamy.")*
- 4 c sliced bananas *(barely ripe)*
- 1 *(12 oz)* box vanilla wafers

Directions

1. In a large mixing bowl, combine the cold milk and pudding mix. Beat with a mixer until smooth and slightly thickened.
2. Add the sweetened condensed milk and stir until fully combined.
3. Gently fold in one container of whipped topping until smooth.
4. In a 9x13-inch dish, layer one-third of the vanilla wafers on the bottom, followed by one-third of the banana slices, and one-third of the pudding mixture.
5. Repeat the layers twice more, ending with the pudding mixture on top.
6. Spread a layer of the remaining whipped topping over the top of the pudding.
7. Garnish with crushed vanilla wafers.
8. Cover and refrigerate for at least 4 hours, or overnight, before serving.

Pecan Cobbler

Ingredients

- 1 stick salted butter, melted
- 1½ c whole pecans
- 1½ c self-rising flour
- 1½ c sugar
- 1 c buttermilk
- 1 Tbsp vanilla extract
- 1½ c brown sugar
- 1 c boiling hot water

Directions

1. Preheat the oven to 350°F.
2. Pour the melted butter into a 9x9-inch baking dish and sprinkle the pecans evenly over the butter.
3. In a medium mixing bowl, combine the flour, sugar, buttermilk, and vanilla extract. Stir until smooth, then pour the mixture evenly over the pecans.
4. Sprinkle the brown sugar over the top of the batter, then carefully pour the hot water over the entire cobbler. (This will create a caramel-like sauce as it bakes.)
5. Bake for 40–50 minutes, or until golden brown and bubbly. The cobbler will appear slightly jiggly when removed from the oven but will thicken as it cools.
6. Serve warm with ice cream or whipped cream.

Ambrosia

Ingredients

- 2 *(8 oz)* containers whipped topping
- 2 c sour cream
- 1 *(20 oz)* can crushed pineapple, well drained
- 2–3 c sweetened shredded coconut
- 2 c miniature marshmallows *(fruit-flavored recommended)*
- 1 *(6 oz)* jar maraschino cherries, drained and chopped
- 1 *(6 oz)* jar whole maraschino cherries, drained *(for topping)*
- 1 *(29 oz)* can mandarin oranges, drained and chopped

Directions

1. In a large mixing bowl, combine the whipped topping, sour cream, and drained pineapple. Stir until well blended.
2. Gently fold in the shredded coconut, miniature marshmallows, chopped maraschino cherries, and chopped mandarin oranges, one ingredient at a time.
3. Mix gently until evenly combined.
4. Pour the mixture into a 9x13-inch serving dish and smooth the top.
5. Garnish with the whole maraschino cherries.
6. Cover and refrigerate for at least 2 hours before serving to allow the flavors to meld.

Butter Pecan Delight

Ingredients

For the Crust

- 1 c all-purpose flour
- ¾ c chopped pecans
- ½ stick (*¼cup*) unsalted butter, melted

For the Filling

- 1½ c packed brown sugar
- ⅓ c self-rising flour
- 2¼ c evaporated milk
- 3 egg yolks, slightly beaten
- 2 Tbsp salted butter, softened
- 1 tsp maple extract

Cream Cheese Layer

- 8 oz cream cheese, softened
- 1 c powdered sugar
- 8 oz container frozen whipped topping, thawed

Directions

Crust

1. Combine the crust ingredients — 1 cup all-purpose flour, ¾ cup chopped pecans, and ½ stick melted unsalted butter — in a bowl.
2. Press the mixture evenly into a 9x13-inch baking dish.
3. Bake at 325°F for about 15 minutes, then let cool completely.

Filling

4. In a medium saucepan, whisk together 1½ cups packed brown sugar, 1/3 cup self-rising flour, 2¼ cups evaporated milk, and 3 slightly beaten egg yolks.
5. Cook over med heat, stirring constantly, until the mixture comes to a boil.
6. Reduce heat to low and continue stirring till it starts to thicken.
7. Remove from heat and stir in 2 tablespoons softened salted butter and 1 teaspoon maple extract.
8. Stir well to combine, then let cool completely.
9. Place a piece of plastic wrap directly on the surface of the filling while it cools to prevent a skin from forming.

Cream Cheese Layer

10. In a medium bowl, beat the cream cheese and powdered sugar until smooth.
11. Fold in the whipped topping until well combined.

Assemble

12. Spread the cream cheese mixture evenly over the cooled crust.
13. Pour the cooled pudding filling over the cream cheese layer.
14. Top with additional whipped topping and sprinkle with chopped pecans.
15. Chill for 4–6 hours before serving.

Mamaw's Homemade Banana Pudding with Meringue Topping

Ingredients

- 3 c evaporated milk or whole milk.
- ¾ c granulated sugar
- 3 Tbsp self-rising flour
- 1½ tsp vanilla extract
- 1 Tbsp unsalted butter, softened
- 4-5 large, almost-ripe bananas, sliced *(or as many as you like)*
- 4 large egg yolks, beaten and at room temperature *(save the whites for the meringue)*
- 1 box vanilla wafers
- ¼ c sugar
- ¼ tsp cream of tartar

Directions

Prepare the Custard

1. In a heavy saucepan over medium heat, combine milk, sugar, and flour.
2. Cook and stir continuously until the mixture begins to bubble, about 2 minutes.

3. Remove from heat. Slowly ladle a little bit of the hot custard into the beaten egg yolks, whisking constantly to "temper" the eggs.
4. Pour the tempered egg mixture back into the saucepan.
5. Return to medium-low heat and cook, stirring constantly, until the custard thickens, about 2 minutes.
6. Remove from heat and stir in the vanilla extract and butter.
7. Let cool to room temperature.

Prepare the Meringue

8. In a mixing bowl, combine the egg whites, cream of tartar, and sugar.
9. Beat on low speed until combined, then increase to high speed and whisk till stiff peaks form.

Assemble the Pudding

10. In a 9x9-inch baking dish, layer sliced bananas on the bottom, followed by a layer of vanilla wafers on top.
11. Pour some of the custard over the top.
12. Repeat the layers until the dish is full, ending with custard on top.
13. Spread the meringue evenly over the pudding.

Bake and Serve

14. Place the dish under the broiler briefly, just until the meringue is golden brown.
15. Serve warm or chill completely before serving.

Watergate Salad

Ingredients

- 1 *(20 oz)* can crushed pineapple, undrained
- 1 *(4 oz)* box instant pistachio pudding mix
- 1 *(8 oz)* container whipped topping *(Cool Whip®)*
- 2–3 c miniature marshmallows *(I use the colorful marshmallows.)*
- ½ c chopped toasted pecans

Directions

1. In a large mixing bowl, combine the crushed pineapple (with juice) and pistachio pudding mix. Stir until well blended.
2. Gently fold in the whipped topping until evenly incorporated.
3. Add the mini marshmallows and mix until combined.
4. Top with toasted pecans.
5. Chill for several hours before serving.

Harvest Fruit Salad

Ingredients

- 1 red apple, unpeeled and chopped
- 1 pear, unpeeled and chopped
- 2–3 fresh mandarin oranges, peeled and segmented
- 1 c dried cranberries
- ½ c chopped pecans
- 1 c chopped red seedless grapes

Dressing

- Juice from ½ large lemon
- ¼ c honey
- Zest from ½ lemon
- ⅛ tsp ground cinnamon

Directions

1. In a large bowl, gently mix the fruit — apple, pear, oranges, cranberries, pecans, and grapes. Set aside.
2. In a separate bowl, whisk together the dressing ingredients — lemon juice, honey, lemon zest, and cinnamon.
3. Pour the dressing over the mixed fruit and toss gently to coat evenly.
4. Cover and chill for 2–3 hours before serving to allow the flavors to blend.

Dirt Pudding

Ingredients

- 1 family-size package Oreos, crushed
- 2 small boxes instant French vanilla pudding *(or white chocolate flavor)*
- 3 c whole milk
- 1 stick unsalted butter, melted
- 1 c powdered sugar
- 8 oz cream cheese, softened
- 1 *(8 oz)* tub whipped topping *(or 2 c whipped cream)*

Directions

1. For the bottom layer, pour half of the crushed Oreos into a bowl and drizzle the melted butter over them. Stir until the crumbs are well coated.
2. Press the mixture evenly into the bottom of a 9x13-inch pan using your fingers. Set aside.
3. In a separate bowl, mix the cream cheese and powdered sugar together till smooth and creamy. Set aside.
4. In another bowl, combine the pudding mixes with the milk and whisk till smooth and slightly thickened.
5. Gradually add the pudding mixture to the cream cheese mixture, mixing till fully combined and smooth.
6. Fold in the whipped topping or whipped cream until evenly blended.
7. Pour the filling over the prepared Oreo crust and spread evenly.
8. Top with the remaining crushed Oreos.
9. Cover and chill for several hours or overnight to set.

I make this for every holiday per request of my family.

CANDIES/FUDGE

Aunt Patty's Peanut Butter (Pinwheels)

Ingredients

- 1 lb box powdered sugar
- 1–2 c additional powdered sugar *(as needed to form a dough)*
- 1 stick unsalted butter, melted
- 3 Tbsp evaporated milk *(add a little more if needed)*
- 1 tsp vanilla extract
- 1 c creamy peanut butter *(or more, to taste)*

Directions

1. In a large bowl, combine 1 pound of powdered sugar, melted butter, and 3 tablespoons of evaporated milk. Stir together, adding just enough milk or extra powdered sugar until a smooth, consistent dough forms.
2. Lightly dust a flat surface with powdered sugar. Place the dough on the surface and roll it out into a square to your desired thickness.
3. Spread the peanut butter evenly over the dough, all the way to the edges.
4. Starting from the side farthest from you, with your fingers, roll the dough tightly toward yourself, tucking it in as you go to form a log.
5. Using dental floss or thread, slice the roll into even pieces.
6. Serve immediately or chill briefly to firm up before serving.

Peanut Butter Fudge

Ingredients

- 2 c sugar
- ½ c evaporated milk
- 3 Tbsp light corn syrup
- 3 Tbsp unsalted butter, softened
- 1 c smooth peanut butter
- 1 tsp vanilla extract

Directions

1. In a heavy saucepan, combine the sugar, evaporated milk, and corn syrup.
2. Place over medium heat, stirring constantly, and bring the mixture to a boil.
3. Continue stirring and cook until the mixture reaches 234°F on a candy thermometer, or until it reaches the soft ball stage.
4. Remove from heat and add the peanut butter, butter, and vanilla extract.
5. Stir till smooth. The mixture will begin to thicken and lose its gloss.
6. Pour into an 8×8-inch dish and let cool completely before cutting into squares.

Divinity

Ingredients

- 2½ c granulated sugar
- ½ c water
- ½ c light corn syrup
- ⅛ tsp salt
- 2 egg whites, room temperature
- 1 c chopped pecans *(optional)*
- 1 tsp vanilla extract

Directions

1. Line a cookie sheet with parchment paper or a silicone baking mat and set aside.
2. In a large saucepan over medium heat, combine the sugar, water, corn syrup, and salt. Stir occasionally until the mixture begins to boil.
3. Clip a candy thermometer to the side of the pan and continue cooking without stirring until the temperature reaches 260°F (about 8–10 minutes).
4. While the sugar mixture cooks, beat the egg whites on high speed in a stand mixer fitted with a whisk attachment until stiff peaks form. Then switch to the paddle attachment.
5. Once the sugar mixture reaches 260°F, remove it from heat. With the mixer running on high speed, slowly pour the hot syrup in a thin, steady stream over the egg whites. This process should take about 2 minutes—go slow, do not rush.
6. Continue beating on high speed for 5–8 minutes, until the candy loses some of its gloss and begins to hold its shape. Test by dropping a small spoonful onto parchment paper; it should

form a mound with soft swirls rather than spreading into a puddle.

7. Continue beating for 1-2 more minutes if the candy does not hold its shape.
8. When the candy holds its shape, mix in the vanilla and chopped pecans (if using).
9. Working quickly while the candy is still hot, use two spoons lightly coated with cooking spray to drop tablespoon-sized scoops of divinity onto the prepared baking sheet. Use one spoon to scrape the candy off the other.
10. Let the candy set completely at room temperature before serving or storing.

Buckeye Fudge (No Boil)

Ingredients

- 1½ c creamy peanut butter
- 1 stick unsalted butter, softened
- 1 tsp vanilla extract
- Approximately 6 c powdered sugar *(use more or less as needed)*
- 1 c chocolate chips *(any kind)*

Directions

1. In a large glass bowl, combine the peanut butter and butter. Microwave for about 1 minute till melted, then stir till smooth.
2. Add the vanilla extract, then mix in the powdered sugar, about 2 cups at a time, until the mixture forms a smooth, dough-like consistency.
3. (Optional) For a creamier texture, drizzle in a small amount of whole milk as needed.
4. Press the mixture evenly into a buttered 8x8-inch dish.
5. Melt the chocolate chips in the microwave in 20-second intervals, stirring between each, until smooth.
6. Spread the melted chocolate evenly over the peanut butter layer.
7. Chill till firm, then cut into squares.

***Tip:** Roll the peanut butter mixture into 1-inch balls, then dip each one into the melted chocolate. Chill until set. --Now you have buckeyes!*

Microwave Chocolate Fudge

Ingredients

- 2 c chocolate chips (*you can substitute sugar-free chips if desired*)
- 14 oz sweetened condensed milk
- ½ stick unsalted butter
- 1 tsp vanilla extract
- 1 c toasted chopped pecans, plus additional for topping

Directions

1. Combine the chocolate chips, sweetened condensed milk, and butter in a medium microwave-safe glass bowl.
2. Heat in the microwave for 90 seconds, then stir to combine.
3. Continue heating in 15-second intervals, stirring between each, till the mixture is melted and smooth. (Note: Microwaves may vary in heating strength, so adjust as needed.)
4. Add the vanilla extract and stir until smooth.
5. Stir in the toasted pecans.
6. Line an 8x8-inch dish with parchment paper. (This makes the fudge easy to remove.)
7. Spread the fudge evenly into the prepared dish and top with additional pecans.
8. Chill for about 3 hours, or till set.
9. Lift the fudge out of the dish using the parchment paper and cut into 1-inch squares.
10. Store covered in the refrigerator to keep the fudge firm.

Cracker Candy (Toffee)

Ingredients

- ½ c brown sugar
- 1 stick unsalted butter, room temperature
- 6 oz milk chocolate chips
- Saltine crackers *(enough to line a baking sheet)*

Directions

1. Preheat the oven to 400°F.
2. Line a 9x13-inch baking dish with saltine crackers in a single layer and set aside.
3. In a heavy saucepan, combine the brown sugar and butter. Cook and stir over medium heat until the mixture comes to a boil.
4. Boil for 1½ minutes, stirring occasionally.
5. Carefully pour the hot mixture evenly over the crackers, spreading it evenly.
6. Bake for about 3 minutes, then remove from the oven.
7. Immediately sprinkle the chocolate chips over the hot toffee and let them sit for 5 minutes to melt.
8. Once melted, spread the chocolate evenly.
9. Chill for 2–3 hours, or until firm, then break apart into pieces before serving.

Fantasy Fudge

Ingredients

- 3 c sugar
- ¾ c butter
- ⅔ c evaporated milk
- 1 package *(12 ounces)* semisweet chocolate chips
- 1 jar *(17 oz)* marshmallow fluff
- 1 c walnuts, chopped
- 1 tsp vanilla extract

Directions

1. Line a 9×13-inch pan with parchment paper and set aside.
2. In a large saucepan over medium heat, combine the sugar, butter, and evaporated milk.
3. Bring the mixture to a boil, stirring constantly. Continue cooking until it reaches 234°F on a candy thermometer (about 5 minutes).
4. Remove from heat and stir in the chocolate chips until melted and thoroughly combined.
5. Add the marshmallow fluff, walnuts, and vanilla extract. Stir till fully incorporated.
6. Pour the mixture into the prepared pan and spread evenly.
7. Allow the fudge to set at room temperature for about 4 hours, or refrigerate to speed up the process.
8. Serve at room temperature.

Old Timey Chocolate Fudge Candy

Ingredients

- 2 c sugar
- 1 c milk
- 1½ c cocoa powder
- ½ c peanut butter *(optional)*
- 3 Tbsp unsalted butter
- 1 tsp vanilla extract

Directions

1. Butter an 8×8-inch dish and set aside.
2. In a medium saucepan, combine the sugar, cocoa, and milk. Stir to blend, then bring the mixture to a boil, stirring constantly.
3. Reduce the heat to low and let simmer. Do not stir again.
4. Place a candy thermometer in the pan and cook until the temperature reaches 238°F.

Tip: *If you don't have a thermometer: drop a small amount of the mixture into a cup of cold water. If it forms a soft ball that flattens when pressed between your fingers, it's ready.*

5. Remove from heat and add the butter and vanilla extract.
6. Beat the mixture with a wooden spoon until the fudge loses its shine and thickens. (Do not underbeat.)
7. Pour into the prepared pan and let cool completely.
8. Cut into about 60 squares and serve.

NOTES

NOTES

NOTES

NOTES

NOTES